Doing
Your
Education
Research
Project

Doing Your Education Research Project

Neil Burton,
Mark Brundrett &
Marion Jones

Los Angeles • London • New Delhi • Singapore • Washington DC

First Published 2008
Reprinted 2008

SAGE Publications Ltd
1 Oliver's Yard
55 City Road
London EC1Y 1SP

SAGE Publications Inc.
2455 Teller Road
Thousand Oaks, California 91320

SAGE Publications India Pvt Ltd
B 1/I 1 Mohan Cooperative Industrial Area
Mathura Road
New Delhi 110 044

SAGE Publications Asia-Pacific Pte Ltd
33 Pekin Street #02-01
Far East Square
Singapore 048763

Library of Congress Control Number: 2007938209

British Library Cataloguing in Publication data

A catalogue record for this book is available from the British Library

ISBN 978-1-4129-4754-1
ISBN 978-1-4129-4755-8 (pbk)

Typeset by CEPHA Imaging Pvt. Ltd., Bangalore, India
Printed in Great Britain by The Cromwell Press Ltd, Trowbridge, Wiltshire
Printed on paper from sustainable resources

Dedications

To George and Val Burton (for making all of this possible through their support and love over the years), Dorothy Brundrett and Bob, Tristan and Kathryn.

Neil Burton, Mark Brundrett & Marion Jones

Contents

Introduction   xi

SECTION 1: Think before you do   1

1: The benefits of practical research   3

The move towards a postgraduate profession   4
Towards research informed practice   6
From teacher to researcher   7
Individualised learning   10
Base-lining and evaluating impact   11
Learning teacher, learning school, learning organisation   13
Learning check   13
Further Reading   15

2: Analysing situations – identifying issues   16

Research with a purpose   17
External influences   19
Internal issues   21
Asking questions   24
Starting points and open minds   25
Clarifying purpose   27
Further Reading   28

3: Reviewing existing ideas   29

Conducting a literature review   30
Conducting a systematic review   32
Making literature reviews more systematic   35
Using the literature review to develop a conceptual framework
for a research study   37
Conclusions   40
Further Reading   41

SECTION 2: Planning and preparation — 43

4: Who to ask — 45

Introduction — 45
Selecting a sample — 46
Probability sampling — 46
Non-probability sampling — 47
Gaining access — 48
The gatekeeper — 49
Ethical issues — 50
Ownership — 52
Balance of power — 54
Informed consent — 56
Conclusion — 58
Further Reading — 58

5: How to ask – decisions, decisions! — 59

Models of research – a philosophical starting point — 59
Approaches to research — 64
Deconstruct the question — 68
Working from pros and cons — 72
Selection or de-selection? — 76
Summary — 77
Further Reading — 77

6: How to ask – surveying the situation — 78

What is a survey? — 79
What is a case study? — 80
Questionnaires and interviews — 80
The delivery format – questionnaires — 81
The delivery format – interviews — 83
Constructing an interview schedule — 86
Interview schedule – the research tool — 88
Constructing a questionnaire — 89
Questionnaire – the research tool — 93
Further Reading — 94

7: How to ask – observing operations and outcomes   95

The 'natural' research tool of the educational profession?	96
Types and forms of observation	97
Research tools and methods of recording data	99
Methods of analysis of observational data	105
Ethics and observational methods	106
Intervention?	107
Conclusions	107
Further Reading	108

8: How to ask – deciphering documentation   109

What is a 'document'?	109
How can documents be used in research activity?	111
Assessing documents	115
Accessing documents	116
Developing documentary research tools	117
Analysing documentary evidence	122
Summary of strengths	123
And weaknesses	123
Further Reading	123

9: How to ask – action research   124

Introduction	124
The nature of 'action research'	125
Definition of action research	127
Identifying the general idea	128
Formulating the research question	130
The action research process	132
Planning your action research project	135
Action research – a constructivist approach to knowledge creation	136
Reporting your action research	138
Caveats	138
Further Reading	139

SECTION 3: Reporting – making sense of the outcomes   141

10: Presenting your findings   143

Relationship between data presentation, data analysis and initial
research questions   143
Qualitative and quantitative data   146
Presenting qualitative data   147
Presenting quantitative data   148
Use of basic statistical tests   153
Summary   158
Further Reading   159

11: Analysing – comparing evidence   160

Data storage and retrieval   160
Types of evidence   162
Maintaining focus and coherence   163
Coding – breaking down and reassembling of data   163
Intricate process of data analysis   167
Enhancing the validity of research outcomes   168
Do the data answer the question?   168
External validation   172
Further Reading   173

12: Conclusions: identifying key findings and recommendations   174

Writing research reports – the importance of structure   175
Scholarly skills – referencing   179
Professional reports to non-specialist audiences   179
Using research outcomes to inform practice   182
Conclusions   187
Further Reading   188

Bibliography   189
Index   200

Introduction

The authors of this book have been supporting educational practitioners planning, performing and analysing research in the field of education for a variety of qualifications over a number of years. Using this experience, we have identified the key stages of the process, from the clarification of initial thoughts and purposes to final submission, in order to support and guide the 'novice' researcher through the important decisions that they need to make. We take the view that those using this book will have developed a range of teaching skills and that they will have an awareness and understanding of the processes that underpin the successful planning, delivery and evaluation and assessment of a learning opportunity. These existing teaching skills will be used to scaffold the development of research skills; enabling a transformation of existing strengths rather than 'starting from scratch'.

In the same way that successful teaching does not start at the point of entry to the classroom (significant levels of information gathering, planning and preparation should (will!) already have taken place), so research activity does not begin with the handing out of a questionnaire. The first section of this book focuses on establishing a reason for the research activity so that appropriate decisions can be made about clarifying the context of the research, the purpose and what is already known. The second part concentrates on the gathering of evidence – what needs to be asked; who will be the key sources of information; and how this information may be collected. All of this is explored taking into account the perspective of the researcher, the purpose of the research and the availability of, and access to, the evidence base to achieve an acceptable compromise between the ideal and the achievable. The final three chapters focus on how the evidence can be used to address the purposes of the research activity through effective presentation and analysis in order to be able to draw valid conclusion on which to base decisions about future actions.

Essentially, this book is based around the concept research for *'research informed decision-making'*:

◆ accessing and evaluating published research to inform your practice; and
◆ learning how to research your own organisation or teaching to improve practice.

In this respect, it is intended for educational professionals who are actively involved in the process of teaching, learning support, educational leadership and organisation within education who wish to undertake research activity both as part of a professional and academic qualification and as a means of self- and organisational improvement.

Neil Burton
Mark Brundrett
Marion Jones
September 2007

Section 1
Think Before You Do

Effective, meaningful, manageable and achievable research doesn't just happen. It is the result of the careful consideration of the context in which you are working in, and is linked to your own inspirations and aspirations. In addition to the careful identification and clarification of your research focus, your success will be based upon your reading around the subject to select from existing ideas and findings in order to be able to confidently determine what should be asked; of whom; and how the evidence might be collected. If you allow yourself to stand back from the process, it should be possible to perceive parallels between planning for research and planning for teaching.

This section of the book explores the initial research planning processes, taking you from the identification of the initial ideas through to the point where you have clarified the purpose of your research and have assimilated the lessons from existing theories and findings from published research.

The Benefits of Practical Research

By the conclusion of this chapter it is anticipated that you will have considered and be able to:

◆ understand how research can be used to inform and improve practice;
◆ understand the value of embedding and evaluating initiatives; and
◆ appreciate the value of the processes of educational research to the school/college practitioner.

This chapter provides an examination of the need, for those working in schools and colleges, to develop and utilise research skills for their own personal professional development and organisational improvement. Whilst this chapter will not tell you *what to do* or *how to do it* (later chapters will do that), it will provide you with an appreciation, hopefully an understanding, of *why*. Developing an understanding of why you are doing something will allow you to gain much more from the activity.

By engaging with new ideas and research findings to develop new practices and evaluate curriculum change, educational practitioners (such as yourself) will be better placed to formalise and enhance personal, and organisational, reflective practice. Excellent teachers improve their effectiveness, that is, how well the learners are learning, by asking the right questions and reflecting on the responses in light of what they have previously experienced and read about, before deciding upon a specific course of action. In many learning environments (classrooms) you may only have a fraction of a second to cycle through these processes. In order to become 'effective', in this sense, it is appropriate to deconstruct these processes, slow them down so that the different elements can be appreciated, valued and practiced. In order to be able to scale down to the micro-decisions, made constantly during a working day, it is appropriate to examine the processes on a much grander scale, to ask 'bigger' questions and formally gather evidence to analyse in order to draw robust conclusions – make the 'right' decisions.

There are an increasing number of pressures on those working in the education profession (and those in training to join!) to become more 'research active' in order to inform and develop their own practice. All phases of education – higher, further and all stages of the maintained sector (primary and secondary) – are not only enhancing the professional and academic credibility of the entry requirements; there is also an increased expectation for the demonstration of the impact for continuing professional development (CPD)

The move towards a postgraduate profession

In the maintained sector, pre-service qualifications are increasingly being delivered and assessed at postgraduate (that is to say 'masters', level), with post-degree level qualifications for entry to the teaching profession changing to accommodate this. In Scotland, at least, you will now be awarded a PGCE (postgraduate certificate of education) for achieving qualified teacher status (QTS) with a masters level award and a PGDE (professional graduate diploma in education) for a purely professional (that is, non-academic) QTS (Souter, 2007). The bodies in England responsible for funding and supporting the quality of CPD provision for teachers, the Training and Development Agency *for schools* (TDA) and the General Teaching Council *for England* (GTC), are both leading the profession towards masters level in service professional development. The TDA, through its subsidisation of masters level study as part of the postgraduate professional development (PPD) initiative is attempting to ensure that school teachers develop the skills to enable them to become more rigorous in the way that they perceive, reflect upon and analyse the impact of educational initiatives that they are involved in. Although significant funding has been made available (TDA, 2007) and tangible professional and financial benefits have been shown to accrue to participants, the uptake is still relatively small. The GTC approach, through the Teacher Learning Academy (TLA) takes a rather more direct approach. In order to progress up the pay spine teachers have to demonstrate their impact within (and beyond!) their school. Level 3 within the TLA criteria (GTC, 2007) equates to masters level study in which teachers are expected to apply appropriately rigorous approaches to gathering and analysing evidence of their 'impact'.

The National College for School Leadership (NCSL) has well established professional qualifications for school leaders, National Professional Qualification for Headship (NPQH), which has now reached such blanket coverage for prospective school leaders that additional qualifications (such as educational masters) to enable employers to distinguish more effectively between the candidates. The qualification for departmental subject leaders, Leading from the Middle (LftM), has also reached a point where holders of the award are expected to convert it into 'academic currency' through gaining accreditation within a masters qualification. Pay and professional progression are increasingly being employed to encourage teachers to develop additional reflective and analytical skills. Within the maintained sector, teaching is increasing moving away from being a graduate profession to becoming a *post*graduate profession.

The post compulsory education (PCE) sector has taken a similar position to the TLA, indeed more so as it also sets criteria for the professional qualities on entry to the profession (SVUK, 2007). At the diploma (level 5) stage, the stated requirements (SVUK, 2007) for accredited programmes are consistent with the research expectations to be found within professional masters courses within education. As a result of the establishment of these national criteria for both pre- and in-service training provision the academic rigour of courses is being more fully recognised in the level of academic award and along with this comes a heightened awareness of the role of research activity as an integral skill development aim for all budding autonomous learners in this sector.

In higher education the role of research activity is complicated by the academic expectations of the sector. Whilst it is acknowledged, as Hattie & Marsh suggest:

> *Universities need to set as a mission goal the improvement of the nexus between research and teaching . . . . The aim is to increase the circumstances in which teaching and research have occasion to meet.* (1996: 533)

The precise nature and focus of this research is less clear. Academics are expected to possess subject expertise within a field of study and to develop this expertise through further study and research, in doing so extending the boundaries of the field and enhancing knowledge within the subject. This 'new' knowledge will then be used to inform the content of their teaching. However, to be an effective teacher of their subject they also need to be aware of, and be able to develop further, the effectiveness of their knowledge/skills transfer to their students. University academics are expected to both be effective researchers within their subject and effective teachers of their subject. Until the establishment of the Institute for Learning and Teaching in Higher Education (ILTHE) the focus for training in higher education was strongly biased towards the research requirements. Currently the Higher Education

Academy (HEA) offers accreditation for courses (HEA, 2007) which support the development of the student learning experience – a pedagogic rather than subject focus. This distinction is crucial when focusing upon the precise nature of research which underpins personal professional development as a teacher (in any phase of education).

Towards research informed practice

Over the past few decades 'research evidence' has increasingly been used by policy makers, nationally and locally, to encourage particular ways of working within education. The educational agenda, from the nature and construction of the curriculum, through approaches to pedagogy to the training and deployment of professionals working in education, is justified and driven by 'best practice' as defined by local, national and international research. Systematic inquiry designed to unveil the 'best' ways of achieving desired outcomes. Research methodology (as opposed to the approach) focuses upon the identification of sources of evidence and how it might be gathered, and is explored in detail in section 2; where issues of *qualitative* and *quantitative* evidence will also be addressed.

The literature on forms of education research is rich in terminology (jargon) which attempts to explain the perspective from which the research is performed (*paradigms* – the research model). In an attempt to obtain clarity and establish lines of demarcation, approaches which would otherwise be seen as complementary are treated almost as incompatible. *Positivism*, which takes an objective perspective of evidence, focusing on the measurement of outcomes in order to predict and identify patterns (Cohen et al, 2007), is made distinct from *interpretive* approaches, which concentrate on interpretation of evidence and bringing meaning. On the whole, research evidence only becomes 'useful' (to individual schools, departments or teachers) when findings are explained, interpreted and contextualised. At a 'research aware' level, this interpretation may be overlaid by the political perspectives of the researcher and the way that they view society and social interaction (for example, Feminist and Marxist research). This 'political perspective' often provides a guide as to how the researcher views and constructs 'knowledge' and is referred to as the *epistemology*.

Reflective practice, which can lead into an action research approach, may be described as *phenomenological*, in that it values the importance of the study of phenomena through direct experience, which is then interpreted and used as the basis for future understanding or modified actions. Smyth (1989) succinctly presents it as a four-stage model:

1. *description* – an evidenced commentary of the current situation;
2. *information* – interpreting the evidence for meaning;
3. *confrontation* – explaining the evidence and the progression to this point; and
4. *reconstruction* – suggesting possible ways of progressing from this point.

For the teacher, there are clear parallels between this model and the reflective teacher model inherent in current school-based education. As a paradigm, it is worthy of further consideration. It does not preclude the adoption of positivist or interpretive approaches, indeed it is enriched by the inclusion, and it also offers some degree of connectivity to approaches which teachers have some familiarity with.

If we accept that research *does* inform practice in the field of education, a focus on the technologies underpinning effective learning and teaching might lead to the reasonable assumption that there will be an emphasis on action research. The implication being that research will inform practice through an iterative process based upon a developing synthesis of theory and practice. In the longer term this may well be an appropriate position to take, but it does imply that all research activity concerning change or improvement must be dynamic in nature and implementation. As teachers we can appreciate that assessment can be for different purposes, but equally valid, the same is true of research. Assessment *for* learning (formative, diagnostic) can immediately be seen as being part of a continuous process. Whereas assessment *of* learning (summative) relates to a specific point within the learning process (and not necessarily an end point). Equally, it would be entirely valid to perform a research activity at any given point within a 'learning' or 'development cycle' in order to, perhaps, determine the most appropriate course of action from a range of alternatives; or to evaluate the impact of an initiative against an appropriate set of success criteria. In each case the research activity is being used at some level to inform a potential future course of action.

From teacher to researcher

Whilst teacher qualification relies upon meeting government determined professional standards, Taber's (2007) 'weak' model of the teaching profession, research proficiency provides it with depth, robustness and a sense of potential future progress. To support this, research should be viewed very much as a process driven activity. Whilst the outcomes of individual research studies are important and can have a significant impact on future actions, the process provides a tool that can become an essential element of a teacher's long-term development aspirations. It is perhaps helpful to begin with a very simplistic comparison of the teaching and researching processes (Fig. 1.1). When contemplating a change it is always worth

Phase	Teaching	Researching
1	Pre-assess the children to ensure that the 'starting point' for learning is revealed and review the National Curriculum documents to clarify expected learning. Establish learning objectives.	Perform a contextual analysis to clarify the issues that the study will focus on and review any relevant national documentation to reveal the wider background and influential factors. Establish key research questions. *What am I trying to find out?*
2	Read subject material (schemes, subject association journals) to collect ideas on how the concepts and skills might be taught and the possible approaches to teaching and learning.	Read the literature on relevant theories to establish a wider conceptual perspective for the study and published empirical research to review potential outcomes and possible methodologies. *What do I already know?*
3	Use contextual knowledge of the group to be taught along with reading of pedagogic texts to establish and clarify the teaching and learning strategies to be employed to meet the learning objectives. Construct the means of assessing learning and record the assessment outcomes.	Use knowledge of the context and research population along with reading from the research methodology literature to establish and clarify the research methodologies to be employed to gather evidence to address the research questions. Construct the research tools. *How can I find out what I need to know?*
4	Evaluate the outcomes of the learning against the expectations of the learning objectives and evaluate the pedagogic qualities of the teaching.	Analyse the outcomes of the research against the key research questions using the theoretical/empirical expectations from the literature. *What have I found out and what does it mean?*
5	Draw conclusions as to the learning that has taken place and the effectiveness of the teaching. Make recommendations for future teaching and learning.	Draw conclusions from the analysis of the research findings. Make recommendations for future action. *So what should I do about it?*

Fig. 1.1 ◆ A simplistic comparison of the teaching and researching processes

identifying the similarities and differences between what you are already doing and what you need to be doing – it is a concept which lies at the heart of formative assessment – assessment for learning (AfL).

Since 'research' is very diverse collection of approaches and frameworks, it is important to offer a restricted perspective of the nature of research to achieve some level of 'manageability', particularly with the novice researcher in mind.

Whilst the model in Fig. 1.1 does not provide exact parallels between the teaching and research processes, there is sufficient connectivity to see it as a starting point for development. Equally, it must be acknowledged, there is not an exact link to Smyth, as Smyth's model relates to a specific point in an otherwise dynamic process – the reflective interlude between period of activity. Indeed, the teaching column is open to question in that it suggests a single learning cycle, but perhaps this is realistic if it assumed that a 'lesson' is made up of a series of learning cycles, some focusing on individuals, some of groups and others on the class as a whole, which is perhaps more representative of the complexities of a lesson format.

Phase 1 holds the key to success; if the lesson (or the research) is ill-founded, the remainder of the process will either be inefficient or flawed. The social constructivist view of teaching holds that we first establish the existing understanding and skills levels of the learners, before constructing the learning opportunity. If the learning is based upon the teacher's assumptions of the learners there is likely to be a degree of mismatch, but as time and resources are clearly a factor in this equation, there needs to be an appropriate balance between assumption and assessment. Similarly, whilst the research needs to establish a clear focus for the research effort it should not attempt to pre-empt the research outcomes. In both cases, reading around the likely issues will enable the teacher/researcher to identify the key factors that need to be addressed – either in terms of the learning or research – so that clear learning or research objectives can be established.

Whilst the wider reading indicated in phase 2, may frequently be sidelined by the experienced teacher, it should be regarded as an essential requirement for both the novice teacher and the novice researcher. For the novice the learning inherent in the process is just as important, in the long term, as any outcomes that may arise.

The third phase focuses on the question 'how will I gather evidence?' – the teacher's question of 'how will I know what they have learnt?', translates as 'how will I know that I've answered my research questions?' for the researcher. In both cases, phase 4 represents a matching of expectations against outcomes using the evidence that is available and the final phase uses this as a basis for future action.

Although it is helpful and possibly reassuring to realise that there are similarities in the process which allow for the possibility of a more successful transfer of skills from one context to the other, it is also important to recognise the differences. It would be all too easy for the experienced educator to fall in to the trap of treating research activity with the contempt of perceived familiarity. As all teachers are individualist in their approaches to teaching and learning (no two lessons, however close the planning, will ever be taught identically) these differences need to be acknowledged and highlighted within the learning processes.

Individualised learning

Whilst learning frequently takes place within a group experience (a class) for reasons of economic, as well as educational, efficiency, this form of collaboration, in addition to the motivational impact, also provides important opportunities to share, trial, test and demonstrate individual learning. It is important to note that this shared learning experience does not need to mean a shared content, indeed there is often more to be learnt from the experience when the group does have slightly different learning needs and interests.

A strength of personal professional development, as an issues-driven research focus, is that it allows for (if not encourages) a collaborative approach to discussing and sharing understanding of the underlying factors. If, for example, 'poor classroom behaviour' is perceived as being a generic issue for the organisation or the group of teachers who are working together which needs to be addressed, the views of teachers should be aired to consider the extent and possible factors impacting on the unwanted behaviour. It then allows different teachers to explore the possible impact of these various factors and contribute to a more informed debate with a view to approaching this through more detailed and differentiated (by context or precise focus) research. As the research activity should be based upon individual and contextual needs, duplication of effort can be avoided with the potential to learn from each other. Even in cases where the conceptual focus (for example, the use of the same behaviour strategy) is the same, the uniqueness of each learning situation (for example, age of class, learning environment or subject area) will individualise the learning experience.

Even without a clear 'personal need', organisational and departmental development plans offer opportunities to identify issues which can used to stimulate both personal and organisational growth. It is also worth noting that this does also offer a wider audience from which to receive feedback and support. It is always worth mapping personal development plans (PDP) and aspirations against the needs of the organisation in order to find areas of joint interest and compatibility which should lead to greater opportunity and access to valuable resources (such as time!)

Base-lining and evaluating impact

Education, due in no small part to the wealth of research evidence driving developments, is rich in new initiatives. All too frequently the 'new' simply overlays existing structures, systems and approaches with only passing regard to the overall compatibility and coherence to those impacted upon. The adoption of new ideas is most effective when a clear 'starting point' is identified to allow a more harmonious co-existence of the current with the new – a meshing rather than a grating. To be confident about accurately identifying the current disposition of the situation (for example, a classroom, subject, department, school), self-evaluation is an essential first step. If you have a destination in mind (the 'new initiative') the journey will be much more successful if you have a clear idea of where you are starting from (again, the parallels with the learning/teaching process should be immediately apparent).

Most incidences of 'change' in educational settings have three distinct opportunities for research activity:

◆ Where are we? (static base-line assessment)
◆ Are we getting there? (dynamic tracking against clear success criteria)
◆ Are we there yet? (dynamic – completion of tracking or static re-establishing of a 'set' position)

For a number of years, schools in England have been driven by school improvement plans (SIPs), policed by centralised inspection regimes (Ofsted) which call on schools to clarify their strengths, weaknesses and goals through self-evaluation forms (SEFs), which are then checked through direct observation. Increasingly the process is driven by a greater reliance on evidence generated within the school with comparisons to wider collations of 'comparative data'. It is the nature of this evidence base and the interpretations that can be placed upon it that offer significant opportunities for personal and organisational development.

For all those operating as teachers within educational settings, all initial training processes are constructed around the concept of self-reflection and personal responsibility for professional development through some form of mentoring or coaching process. But whether the focus for development is on the organisation of the individual, research activity is at the heart of the process. For this reason alone it can be appreciated that the value of developing educators in the skills of researchers is not a purely academic exercise to give credibility to training programmes, but rather an essential skill necessary for the future development of the education sector and the professionalism of those working in it. Whilst it is acknowledged that the delivery of effective learning may be placed into the competent hands of education technicians such as high level teaching assistants or trainers, teachers are increasingly being required to rely upon skills developed through contextually focused research activity in order to accurately assess a situation, choose an appropriate course of action and evaluate the impact. These skills, which can be honed in the learning environment, are becoming an essential for those in and aspiring to educational leadership.

Essentially making changes to the learning environment or the wider organisation requires a significant investment in resources, time in particular. So before doing anything particularly drastic it is worthwhile establishing a precise need to ensure that any initiative that may be implemented is appropriate to the need, addresses perceived weaknesses and builds upon strengths and areas of confidence. A well directed research activity should establish that what is thought to be the problem does not, in reality, turn out to be simply a symptom of a bigger issue.

Frequently organisations have little control over the initiatives that they are required to adopt and fail to invest time in gaining an understanding. This lack of knowledge can lead to a superficiality in the approach and result in poorly constructed implementation. By engaging with the research underpinning the initiative, ownership can be taken leading to greater personal and organisational investment. This can be further supported by constructing research informed tools for tracking the implementation process.

Learning teacher, learning school, learning organisation

The concept of the learning organisation is not new but is quite fitting for the education sector, being, as it is, in the 'business' of education. All those working in the education sector should be focused on the learning of their students (admittedly, there may be a dual focus in the case of universities) and to best achieve and maintain this emphasis, everybody within those organisations must continuously focus on their own learning. The successful adaptation to change and uncertainty, which schools and colleges strive for, is most likely to occur when sufficient and appropriate learning takes place throughout the organisation.

Although research activity can only ever claim to be part of a range of learning opportunities, its impact can be significant. It can be used to identify specific needs in oneself and others, and also to explore deficiencies and untapped potentials. Professionally focused inputs (such as 'tricks for teachers' forms of CPD) can be embedded and their longer term impact on educational quality evaluated. Links between processes, skills and strategies applied to the learning environment and the wider organisational needs can be identified and developed (for example, linking strategies for motivating staff and students) to offer a more coherent approach.

Above all else, research activity makes you think more deeply about what you are doing, to evaluate impact and applicability, and to consider alternative options. By encouraging a more healthily sceptical view of innovation it is possible to develop within the professional staff a more enduring and robust capability for change.

Learning check

An important question to ask is − 'what is your motivation for developing your educational research skills?' As we see with our own learners, the more that they can see a purpose for the learning and can appreciate its applicability to their wider needs, the more highly motivated they will be. Whilst there will always be some element of 'learn it for the test' within education, the superficiality of this approach and the transitory nature of that learning in our memory is often a woeful waste of effort in the longer term. Those who learn and apply research skills as part of their initial professional development for the education profession will perhaps need

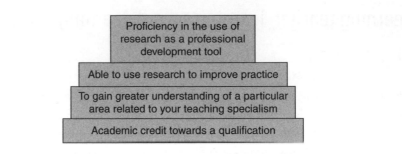

Fig. 1.2 ◆ Levels of engagement with research activity

to focus on embedding and developing the core technical skills in the early part of their career and may not perceive research activity as a crucial aspect of their own early progression.

Figure 1.2 offers a hierarchal means of viewing your own engagement with the importance and applicability of the research process. There is likely to be a base line of completion of academic credit, but this really needs to be perceived as a reward or acknowledgement of competence that is a goal in itself. At the lowest level of effective engagement it may simply be considered as a tool to access a more secure understanding of a particular aspect of teaching or learning (or educational management) which is relevant and specific to your individual needs at this point in time.

Using research to improve practice can be viewed in two ways. First in terms of being able to engage constructively with published research through having sufficient understanding of the process to be able to critically review findings. Second in terms of being research active and being competent in the use of a narrow range of skills which enable you to track your own progress and development and challenge yourself through the incorporation of a wider range of ideas gained through reading. In effect, a fully committed reflective practitioner, through the use of action research methodologies.

Ideally the value of research as a tool for learning will be such that you will consider it as a primary choice and a means of driving and support your own personal development and the development of your organisation.

FURTHER READING

◆ Denscombe, M., *The Good Research Guide* (2nd Ed) Maidenhead: Open University Press (2003)

◆ Hopkins, D., *A Teacher's Guide to Classroom Research*, Maidenhead: Open University Press (2002)

◆ Middlewood, D., Cloleman, M. and Lumby, J. (Eds), *Practitioner Research in Education: Making a Difference*, London: Sage Publications (1999)

◆ Opie, C., *Doing Educational Research*, London: Sage Publications (2004)

◆ Taber K., *Classroom-based Research and Evidence-based Practice*, London: Sage Publications (2007)

 # Analysing Situations – Identifying Issues

This chapter will concentrate on explaining the importance of clarifying the context of the external and internal environments faced by the researcher, in order to be able to identify the key issues that are worthy of research. Specifically, by the completion of this chapter, you should:

◆ be able to identify and clarify an explicit focus for research; and
◆ have considered the local and national factors which impact upon classroom, departmental or organisational practice.

Having addressed some of the issues surrounding why research activity is so important for the individual professional development and organisational health of those working in education, here we focus on making a secure start to your endeavours by identifying an issue to research. All too frequently, novice researchers, particularly those completing a research task in order to obtain an academic award, approach the process with a set of preconceptions which act as constraints on the research design process. A starting point will often be the adoption of a 'research design' (Hitchcock and Hughes, 1995:79), such as action research or survey, rather than the purpose or focus of the research. It is rather like a teacher deciding to use 'small group discussions' and then thinking about what the students need to learn. Section 2 of this book will show the importance of matching the research methodology to the focus and the context of the research. The processes by which evidence might be collected will be subject to both real and perceived constraints – and before deciding on a particular approach it is important to identify what those constraints might be! However, research activity should not be considered as simply being driven by constraints, the researcher should be aware of potential opportunities, from both national and local imperatives. By aligning research activity with a current national initiative' (there are usually so many to choose from) or to an issue identified within an organisational or departmental development plan, the research is likely to receive more support and encounter less resistance.

This chapter will explore how you can achieve the difficult balance of identifying an opportunity for research activity which has the potential to reveal important and meaningful outcomes, whilst at the same time being manageable and achievable.

Research with a purpose

As far as this book is concerned, the purpose of research is to gather and analyse appropriate evidence on which to base decisions to bring about change – preferably improvement. In order to successfully achieve that outcome it is important to analyse the situation you find yourself in, in order to identify the 'right' questions to ask. In effect, you will be carrying out research to clarify what you need to focus your research on. Partially this requires 'reading around' the issues in order to appreciate the current perceptions and to familiarise yourself with the terminology and the key conceptual constructions and theoretical perspectives (read on to chapter 3 for more on how to achieve this). But most importantly it is the context in which you will be performing the research that will most directly provide the opportunities and stimulus.

Whilst there are several texts on research methodology, such as Denscombe (2003), which identify the purpose as being the major driving force behind the construction of the research activity, the emphasis tends to focus on the various means of collective evidence. Even where planning frameworks for research activities are offered (Cohen, Manion and Morrison, 2007), which acknowledge the crucial importance of 'a clear statement of the problem' (p 79) or purpose and go on to suggest links between overarching purposes and research methodologies (p 84–6), the primacy of the methodology is apparent. But how do you arrive at the purpose? All too often, the asking of the 'right question' is the hardest part of getting to the answer.

In an environment which is often driven by 'targets', actual goals are frequently difficult to define or measure so that 'indicators' are identified as a more measurable alternative. This can lead to an overemphasis on short-term measurable gains against indicators rather than concentrating on the core factors which these indicators, indicate. For example, attendance rates are a prime example of an indicator which can confuse and distort strategic thinking. Educational organisations have been known to offer financial bribes to encourage learners to attend rather than explore the potential underlying factors which result in the non-attendance (for example, fear, inappropriate curriculum, financial loss – of possible earnings, is only one of many), so there is a concentration on the symptoms rather than the causes. When faced with a concern such as 'low attendance', a researcher may ask the question 'why?' and gather evidence to identify a possible root cause, or be presented with a preferred solution (a financial bribe to the learner) and asked to provide evidence to determine 'will it work?'.

It is likely that you will be set some artificial constraints as a consequence of a qualification or an award – the issue that is to be at the heart of the research may be restricted to specific aspects of education, such as 'assessment', 'special educational needs' or 'behaviour management'; or by subject area or age/phase or location within an organisational hierarchy. Whatever the imposed focus, it is important to examine how this might relate to the context in which you will be working and researching. By making the research specific to your development needs as well as those of your host organisation, you immediately widen the audience for your research outcomes and give it a purpose beyond the qualification alone.

The process is one of funnelling to get from the possible to the probable; to arrive at a clear and specific focus which your research will be related back to at all stages of the research activity. The first of these is to explore the wider influences on the specific area of educational activity, particularly those determined and driven by government policy. If you are in a complete quandary it might be helpful to start with a review of the key issues that are present in the educational press. Key sources to explore would be:

◆ *The Times Educational Supplement* (*TES*) (www.tes.co.uk)
◆ BBC education news (http://news.bbc.co.uk/1/hi/education/default.stm)
◆ *The Times Higher Educational Supplement* (*THES*) (www.thes.co.uk)

Case Study 2.1 Investigating the factors behind the failure of A/B grade passes at A level to rise inline with overall passes at the school

---

Secondary Head of Faculty (MA student) 'Jon'
Constraint: study must focus on 'curriculum management'

The 13–18 age range school had experienced a trend of rising rates A level passes in line with the national averages, but passes at A/B grades was well below this average. Government documentation pointed towards a more inclusive approach to 16+ education, but also the need to address attainment of the most able students. School data suggested that the more able were under achieving, particularly the boys, but why? Jon wanted to explore the possible causes to the discrepancies:

What opportunities are provided within the school for students to achieve the higher grades?

What are the key motivators for the staff and students and how is this translated into learning habits?

Does the nature of the curriculum meet the learning needs of the students?

External influences

One of the key benefits of having an interventionist government, in respect of educational policy, is that it offers a literature-rich starting point for almost any aspect of educational research that you could imagine, whatever phase of education might be the focus. Whilst the general list of recent Government proposals, papers and proclamations (and reports of funded research projects) is to be found at the Department for Education and Skills (DfES, 2007) website, more specialised documents can be found on the Internet sites of other quasi-governmental organisations. The main repository for documents concerned primarily with classroom-based issues within schools is Teachernet (2007), although there are also links to documents aimed at school leaders, to supplement the wealth of information that is available from the

National College for School Leadership (NCSL, 2007a). As a result of the schools inspection process, Ofsted has become an excellent source of data on performance trends through a collation and aggregation of individual school inspection reports, but it also offers tools for school self-evaluation and tracking pupil achievement (Ofsted, 2007) which might be of use to an education-based research later in the planning and preparation process. Her Majesty's Inspectorate of Education (HMIe, 2007) publish reports which offer an overview of education practice within the different phases.

There are a considerable number of different sources for information in respect of the curriculum that schools are required to deliver and assess, which provide a setting for research into the nature, structure and assessment of the curriculum and the associate learning and teaching. Just to provide examples for the English curriculum gives some idea of the scope and range:

◆ programmes of study and attainment targets (NC, 1999);
◆ implementing the curriculum (Standards, 2007); and
◆ assessment and qualifications (QCA, 2007).

Plus various associated sources which provide guidance and direction on aspects of pedagogy and resources for learning and teaching which are provided to support the implementation and assessment of the curriculum and, inevitably, have a major influence on the nature of learning and teaching in schools and subsequent phases of education.

The sheer scale of this guidance, which determines the environment in which teachers operate, suggests, according to Taber (2007) an '*implicit* mistrust of teachers using their professional judgement' (p 5) – which takes us into the 'guidance' for training and development of teaching professionals. As indicated in the previous chapter, each major phase of education has its own entry requirements and 'gatekeepers' which are quasi-governmental organisations. In teacher education, this role is fragmented between different bodies:

◆ Training and Development Agency for schools (TDA, 2007) that focuses on the recruitment and development of the workforce in schools and controls the funding for award bearing training.
◆ General Teaching Council for England (GTC, 2007) that serves as guardians of the standards for the profession and provides a training framework for the professional development of teachers.

◆ National College for School Leadership (NCSL, 2007b) who commission and provide training for leadership roles within schools.

However, with the Every Child Matters (ECM) agenda (DfES, 2005), there is a much broader spectrum of identifiable influence impacting, in definable ways, on the operation of classrooms and schools which will, perhaps, need to be taken into account. It is only once we begin to place the actions of the school, department, teacher or learner into this wider context that we can begin to appreciate and understand why things happen the way they do. Issues which are regarded as 'important' on the national scale, such as meeting the individual needs of learners in the PCE sector (Niace, 2007), can then, at the very least, be justified much more successfully at the local level. The perspective offered by the national source will often provide an overview of the key factors and so offer a rationale for the closer examination of the local context. On the whole, national initiatives are usually supporting by robust justification which can be used to provide meaning to small-scale, localised research activities.

It is particularly useful, if the research activity needs to be sanctioned by senior leaders within an organisation, if only to pay the fees, if the focus can be linked to a national initiative that the organisation is committed to working towards. It is when the leadership within the organisation can see the wider application of the outcomes of any research that they will be more inclined to support the activity through some material means or by providing access to information.

These national issues often provide a very great influence on the direction that research activity will take. For example, 75% of a cohort of primary-phase undergraduate trainee teachers recently chose AfL as the focus for their dissertations – but there was not one duplication, because each was uniquely located within its own context: age group; subject area; aspect of assessment; assessment tool; breadth of evidence base and so on.

Internal issues

Whilst a general search though the national perspective will identify the potential BIG issues that education is currently being required to address, it is only through an examination of the context in which the research is likely to be carried out that will determine whether the research themes are possible. In many respects, the review of 'internal' and 'external' issues needs to be performed concurrently – top down and bottom up to meet somewhere in the middle. It is the balancing act that most teachers have to master every time they enter the classroom – the set requirements of the curriculum against the needs of the individual learners. Here it is an awareness of the importance of relative wider issues mapped against the priorities of the class, teacher, department or school. One can be used to validate and enhance the importance of the other when agreement to perform the research is being sought.

To a very large extent, the approach that you can take to identify potential research topics depends upon your *positionality* in respect of the research context. Positionality being your relationship to the context and the potential research population. For example, being a newly qualified teacher (NQT), your relationship to the research population, access to information and personal biases will be very different if you decide to gather evidence of your senior leadership team's ability to perform effective self-assessment rather than the ability of the students in your Year 8 tutor group. Similarly, if you are already working in the organisation, you are likely to have a greater awareness of the issues which are deemed to be important or priorities, than if you are simply using it as a source of research evidence. This difference throws up different strategies that prospective research may need to adopt in order to gain access to potential sources of evidence. Whichever of the strategies you employ, it is important that the research topic holds a real interest for you and that it offers the possibility of meaningful gains for you not just in terms of the qualification (if any is on offer!) but also in terms of your personal and professional growth.

In order to identify potential research topics, it is helpful to explore possibilities – informally seeking the views of colleagues and peers about issues that appear important to you and perhaps in the national perspective as well. These anecdotal responses will hopefully give you some sense of direction and help you to select a more precise focus to examine the possibilities of in greater depth. You do need to take care that you don't take it too far – in effect, you are looking for questions, not the answers at this stage.

But what actually is *the* issue that you should be focusing upon? Sometimes it is difficult because you will be given a focus – either because it is an issue that the organisation wants you to research (making *their* priority *your* priority) or because it is given in the form of an assignment focus. In the first instance it is at least likely that you will receive appropriate support and resources from the organisation, in the second, it might take a little more effort to convince your host that your priority becomes one of theirs!

1. *Researching in your own organisation*

   Depending on your length of service and your position within the organisation, it is likely that you will be aware of organisational or departmental priorities which you might be able to embed your research activity within. It is also possible to use your own performance management targets as a focus for your research activity. If you can demonstrate to your line manager the connections between the priorities and your research goals then there is a much greater likelihood of being supported and being given access to appropriate sources of evidence. However, in most circumstances it is likely that you will be faced with a number of competing, seemingly equal priorities. Even taking account of the views of peers and colleagues may not take you much further towards your research focus. At this point you should consult with your line manager, mentor or research supervisor in order to try to obtain a more objective perspective of the options that you have open to you. Ideally, this will continue to include a balance of the organisation's and your own personal priorities.

2. *Researching in a host organisation*

   This is more likely the case if you are performing the research as part of an initial teacher training/education programme which is not wholly school or college-based. Here it is best to approach the organisation with potential research projects which are seen as being based on 'important' issues from the national perspective. If the research is to be tied into a period of classroom/teaching experience, the greater the 'self-focus' and the more contained around your own teaching, the more acceptable it is likely to be. If it is to be completed by taking on the role of 'researcher', then it is important to confirm that the host is sympathetic to the aims, at the very least, but ideally it will focus on something that the hosts themselves see the benefit of. Where both the research and the host are likely to benefit from the activity, there is a greater likelihood of the research being given wider access to evidence and resources by the host.

Case Study 2.2 Design Technology and as a model of AfL

Primary BEd Student 'Jenny'

Constraint: study must focus on your 'specialist subject' (design technology)

The 4–9 age range school that Jenny had been placed in for her final teaching experience were grappling with the problem of getting Key Stage (KS) 1 children to successfully self- and peer-assess. Jenny had noticed the similarities between the AfL and design processes. Trawling government reports

Continued

and curriculum documentation made the connections more apparent and also reinforced the importance of pupil involvement in AfL. School documentation also highlighted the priority of the issue. With this as justification, Jenny identified two key questions:

Can KS1 children be taught how to self- and peer-assess using the design process as a model?

Can they successfully transfer this skill to other areas of the curriculum?

Asking questions

There is an art and a science to asking questions. The best teachers are very expert in this – they have to be in order to get to the heart of misconception, misunderstanding or 'block' that a student is having to learning. By deconstructing the 'problem' they are adept at getting down to a firm foundation in order to help a learner reconstruct a more successful understanding. At the beginning of a research activity it is important for a researcher to progress through a similar process. It is all too easy for a teacher to 'assume' that they know the problem that a learner is having; that is, choosing a starting point which fits their ready made solution – a researcher is capable of doing something very similar. They begin the research with an outcome in mind and tend to collect evidence which supports their idea. Asking questions should help to keep the research 'honest' by focusing down to the key or fundamental issues.

Questioning should be seen as the process by which you get from the important general (but probably amorphous) theme to the manageable specific research focus. Sometimes it is possible to achieve this simply by self-analysis but to avoid missteps due to unacknowledged internal bias, lack of objectivity or positionality (the location of the researcher in respect of the focus of the research), it is often helpful (if not explicitly required!) to discuss the broad focus of the research with a mentor, coach tutor or line manager in order to obtain a different perspective.

Is it just me or do we have a problem here? As well as asking 'those with power over your research' it is also helpful to informally/anecdotally seek to views of peers and colleagues as to the appropriateness of your study.

◆ What do you think about?
◆ Do you find a problem/helpful/challenging/too time consuming?
◆ What do you think we should do about? (which does have the bias of assuming that there is some inherent/acknowledged pre-existing problem)

By obtaining a wider range of views prior to fully formulating an approach or even finalising the focus, it does allow the study to settle towards a position of 'least resistance' or even greatest support, which should have a significantly positive impact on the research processes, particularly in the willingness of colleagues to contribute and participate in any evidence gathering.

Whilst some sources, such as Hitchcock and Hughes (1995:81) offer a simplified framework for establishing a focus for the research, others (Cohen *et al*, 2007; Denscombe, 2003) rather bypass this stage of the process. It is left to more recent publications, including Fox, Martin and Green (2007) and Taber (2007) to adopt a more holistic approach and consider the need to filter down to the key focus. Walliman (2005) adopts the pragmatic approach of identifying the focus (the 'what') before moving onto the justification (the 'why'), although there is an undeniable element of 'chicken and egg' here.

Starting points and open minds

In the role of a tutor, coach or mentor my biggest concern at the initial planning stage is not for the researcher who comes in saying 'I don't know what to do', but the one who says 'our school/class needs to do' – and then state the outcome of the research. Performing research to gather evidence to justify a decision already made might be appropriate in some circumstances, but it does immediately close down the possibilities of what could be 'better' options. 'Intuition' or 'experience' will often lead a teacher to seek (and expect) a particular 'answer' which reinforces their view of reality. This reflects a closed system where only a limited range of options is possible, whereas a research activity should grasp the opportunity to explore the new and consider alternatives.

A clear distinction should be drawn between the prejudging of outcomes, reinforced by a biased approach to the research in which conclusions and the resultant actions are already decided and an objective testing of a hypothesis (positivistic research). The first approach innately attempts to confirm currently held beliefs, the second attempts to challenge those beliefs. To be able to effectively challenge currently held views it is important to acknowledge what they are (a further component of positionality) to establish a personal starting point for a potential 'learning journey'.

However, there is no requirement to begin a research activity with a firmly held set of views! It is quite acceptable to simply identify an issue and explore it, allowing your views to be driven by the reading and the evidence.

Case Study 2.3 Evaluating the effectiveness of the mentoring for a graduate primary, employment-based, initial teacher training programme.

Training manager, primary teacher and MA Education student 'Jo'
Constraint: study must focus on 'performance management'

Jo manages a school-based teacher training programme which relies exclusively on mentoring of the trainees to support their development towards QTS. All the mentors are primary teachers and have been trained to support the trainee teachers using specific structures and strategies. Whilst all trainees who have completed the programme in the past three years have been successful it is not clear which particular elements have contributed most.

In discussions with the tutor, the difficulty in defining 'effective' became apparent, particularly in considering the perceptions of the different interested parties. The decision rested upon the purpose to which the outcomes might be put – to be incorporated within a self-assessment for public consumption a purposive (quantitative) approach would be preferable, but to inform future practice, especially recruitment and training of mentors, a phenomenological (qualitative) approach would be more useful. Choosing a developmental purpose gave the research a specific focus, perspective and direction.

Clarifying purpose

Reading around the subject and exploring the context (national and local background) increases your awareness of the range factors that impact on your study (see Fig. 2.1). From this wider understanding of the issues a precise focus and purpose for the study can then be more confidently established. The purpose is of crucial importance to the success of your study as it should require you to convince yourself why you are doing it before you have to convince any one else to help you collect evidence. It is the opportunity to make explicit the focus you have chosen and to distil this focus into a select number of key research questions that can then be used to establish and maintain the direction of the study throughout the subsequent stages – keep checking your progress and focus against them.

There is an important 'reality check' that needs to be considered as the purpose of the study begins to form; based around the achievability of the proposal.

◆ Ethics – (addressed in greater detail later in respect of evidence gathering processes and reporting of findings) – can any potential risks, in terms of the physical, emotional, financial or general well being of the potential participants or stakeholders, be prevented or minimised?

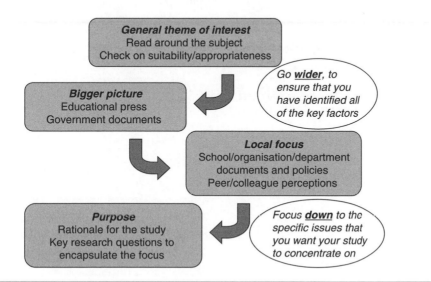

Fig. 2.1 ◆ Establishing a focus

◆ Resources – do you have the time, skills, financial means (for example, travel, phone calls, photocopying) to successfully complete the research?
◆ Access – are you likely to be able to gain access to the key sources of information and evidence necessary to address the key research questions?
◆ Scope – is the depth, range and scale of the research appropriate for my expected level of activity and engagement?
◆ Benefit – are the outcomes of this research likely to be of professional benefit to you or your institution?

If you are able to give a confidently positive response to each of these, it is time to explore the conceptual literature and published research underpinning the study in greater depth.

FURTHER READING

◆ Burton, N., and Brundrett, M., *Leading the Curriculum in the Primary School*, London: Paul Chapman Publishing (2005)

◆ Denscombe, M., *The Good Research Guide* (2nd Ed) Maidenhead: Open University Press (2003)

◆ Fox, M., Martin, P. and Green, G., *Doing Practitioner Research*, London: Sage Publications (2007)

◆ Taber K., *Classroom-based Research and Evidence-based Practice*, London: Sage Publications (2007)

◆ Walliman, N., *Your Research Project*, London: Sage Publications (2005)

Reviewing Existing Ideas

This chapter will discuss some of the key issues in conducting literature searches, outline the increasingly popular, and linked, research approach embodied in the systematic study, and then go on to suggest ways of making all studies more systematic in order to construct a clear conceptual framework for research. Specifically, by the completion of this chapter, you should:

◆ be able to identify a conceptual focus for the study;
◆ appreciate the need to consider the ideas, concepts and strategies suggested by previous authors;
◆ appreciate the applicability of the findings of published research in the field; and
◆ be able to justify the key issues that need to be explored and addressed.

Conducting a high quality review of existing ideas is probably the most important element of any successful research study in the Social Sciences and education in particular. However, this is not universally the case, because occasionally researchers will undertake 'blue skies' research that is at the cutting edge of development and, by inference, there will be very little material available on the topic under scrutiny. However, such circumstances are very rare since it is unusual to find a topic that has been completely unexplored in the past – and unlikely to be the focus of a research activity by a novice researcher. Even issues that may seem to be very new indeed are unlikely to be entirely without antecedents and a determined and thorough review of the literature will almost always reveal a wealth of relevant material that the researcher can draw on in carrying out their study. This chapter will guide you as to how to approach a literature search to identify and critically examine key conceptual and empirical sources available.

The process of conducting literature reviews has been revolutionised by the increasing, and now ubiquitous, use of electronic database searches that enable the researcher to interrogate vast amounts of literature with speed and with ease.

However, even the best and most user-friendly of databases pose certain challenges to the researcher. The very size of the database is often problematic since the insertion of a keyword may produce thousands of responses that place the researcher in little better position than if they still relied on manual examination of card indexes and published summaries of research material according to topic. The researcher still needs to acquire a series of key skills that will enable any search to be carried out successfully and in a way that will refine the amount of material to a manageable level.

Conducting a literature review

A literature review is an account of what has been published on a topic by other researchers. All forms of publication outlet may be used in such a review but special weight is placed on research based text, sometimes termed *research monographs*, and articles published in peer reviewed journals. At their simplest, a review of the literature on a topic may consist of little more than the collation of evidence based on a few minutes spent exploring one particular database, or electronic catalogue search, using only one or two key words. Such an approach is perfectly acceptable if the aim is to find some initial material on an issue of interest. Such a process may also be invaluable in the initial stages of a research study since it can serve a number of key functions including:

◆ Provide information as to whether the topic is one that has been explored in detail already or whether there is a paucity of research on the topic and thereby assist in the decision whether or not to pursue that line of enquiry.
◆ Gathering initial material that will form the basis for further exploration.
◆ Act as a 'framing exercise' to set up the parameters of study by discovering the range of literature and the current state of research and thinking on a topic.

However, one must differentiate between a search and a review. The search is the process of accessing and retrieving data whereas the review is the product of the analytical process that is undertaken consequent on one or more searches. As such the review must be defined by a guiding concept such as the main research problems, aims or questions. Birley and Moreland, (1998: 90) suggest that the researcher must always keep in mind their original aims when conducting a review and provide the helpful mnemonic: *AIM – Author's Intended Message*, as a way of ensuring that original goals are never lost from sight throughout the process.

Such a review must not be just a descriptive list or summary of the material available, it should:

◆ synthesise;
◆ analyse; and
◆ present a clear line of argument.

The latter is probably the most difficult to accomplish, especially for the emerging or new researcher since such argument should never be solely the unsupported views of the research but should rather be a consistent line of argument consonant with the researcher's views *but based on the evidence*. In order to ensure this is accomplished a number of key questions need to be asked by the researcher, such as:

◆ What is the specific thesis, problem or research question that my literature review helps to define?
◆ What type of literature review am I conducting? Am I looking at issues of theory? Methodology or policy?
◆ Am I interested in outputs based quantitative research, qualitative research or the development of theory?
◆ What is the scope of my literature review? What types of publications am I using (for example, journals, books, government documents, popular media)?
◆ What discipline am I working in (for example, nursing psychology, sociology, medicine) and which databases (and increasingly, websites) will be most relevant?
◆ Have I critically analysed the literature? Do I follow through a set of concepts and questions, comparing items to each other and the ways they deal with them? Instead of just listing and summarising items, do I assess them, discussing strengths and weaknesses?
◆ Have I cited and discussed studies contrary to my perspective?
◆ Will the reader find my literature review relevant, appropriate and useful?
◆ How does this book or article relate to the specific thesis or question I am developing?

(University of Melbourne, 2007a)

The resultant literature review should be a piece of discursive prose, not a list describing or summarising one piece of literature after another. Instead, organise the literature review into sections that present a thematic overview or identify trends in relevant theory (Taylor and Proctor, 2007). A good literature review will have a clear rationale for structure and presentation that can be traced back to the nature of the study. One of the simplest ways to provide logical structure is by examining the key research questions, aims or issues and attempting to define a theme that can be pursued in the literature which can then be the subject of a specific search or set of searches and can be reported as one section in the review. However, not all research issues are susceptible to the development of such a theme and some researchers choose to allow the structuring themes to emerge as material is searched. Overall, the paramount issue is to ensure that the structure of the review follows a logical and defensible pattern (this is especially true for doctoral students or those conducting funded research who may have to defend the way that they have presented their material in a viva, interview or presentation to a funding agency).

Ask yourself

What is the overarching concept or issue that underpins your study?

What are the key research questions/aims/or sub-issues that develop out of this?

What are four or five key themes that you need to explore in more detail?

Which key words are the most likely to produce relevant material when you undertake a literature search for each theme?

How might you combine those words in order to explore the issues in more depth and to exclude extraneous results?

Conducting a systematic review

The notion of conducting a systematic review of the literature as part of research study, or even as the principle methodological approach in its own right, has grown significantly in recent years. There are a number of reasons for this:

1. The importation of the systematic review approach from biological and medical sciences in the social sciences.
2. The growing recognition of the importance of a systematic search of previously published studies as a way of creating a conceptual framework of further research.
3. The increasing ability to interrogate enormous amounts of extant literature because of easy access to electronic database searches.

4. The introduction of new frameworks of qualifications such as professional Masters and Doctoral degree programmes within which a systematic literature review may be undertaken as a discrete element of a degree.

Critical appraisal and synthesis of research findings in a systematic manner emerged in the 1970s under the term 'meta-analysis' in the areas of psychotherapy and medicine. The Evidence for Policy and Practice Information (EPPI-Centre 2007) was subsequently established in 1993 to address the need for a systematic approach to the organisation and review of evidence-based work on social interventions and has subsequently become highly influential in the growth of systematic review as an accepted method. The EPPI-Centre 2007 approach argues that the key features of a systematic review or systematic research synthesis are that:

◆ explicit and transparent methods are used;
◆ it is a piece of research following a standard set of stages; and
◆ it is accountable, replicable and updateable.

(EPPI-Centre 2007, 2007a)

A systematic review is different from a traditional literature review precisely because it attempts to be more systematic in its approach. Some of the key ways in which this is achieved include:

◆ Systematic reviews are *transparent* about how their conclusions are generated. Each piece of research is evaluated and its quality and relevance made clear.
◆ A *protocol* sets out how the review is to be conducted before the work starts that is designed to reduce bias.
◆ *Exhaustive searches* are undertaken to find as much as possible of the relevant research in an effort to find as much as possible of the research which addresses the review's research question. This is important if the review's conclusions are not to be over-influenced by studies which are simply the easiest to find (usually published research, showing the benefit of interventions).
◆ Systematic reviews use a set of explicit statements, called *inclusion criteria*, to assess each study found to see if it actually does address a review's research question.
◆ *Potential users of the review are involved* to make sure that the research is relevant through the use of advisory groups.
◆ The *findings of sound research are synthesised* to produce clear and easily accessible messages about the reliable evidence available on a given topic by appraising individual studies and pooling results.

This latter point is one of the most important characteristics of a systematic review; it includes a synthesis of its results usually presented in the form of a structured narrative, summary tables or a statistical combination (meta-analysis). This synthesis is then used to formulate conclusions and recommendations (EPPI-Centre 2007, 2007b). Some systematic maps can be in-depth with a large degree of analysis of the research field. Syntheses are nearly always in depth, as detailed scrutiny of the available research is necessary to be clear about the trustworthiness of that research and the relevance and direction of the findings. This time-consuming, but essential, activity means that systematic reviews including a synthesis often answer a more narrowly focused question. Reviews asking complex questions may be theory testing reviews using more iterative methods of review such as in critical interpretive and realist synthesis (EPPI-Centre 2007, 2007c).

Once searches have been carried out, electronic records of the results can be downloaded from databases and imported into reference management software such as EndNote found at http://www.endnote.com/ or Reference Manager from http://www.refman.com/. More detailed information on studies may be held in a bespoke database constructed by the researcher or research team or a commercial software solution, for example, MsAccess. Equally, analysis of the results of searches may be carried out manually or may use systems such as NVivo (http://www.qsrinternational.com/products_nvivo.aspxand) or NUD*IST (http://www.qsrinternational.com/) (EPPI-Centre 2007, 2007d).

The synthesis needs to be presented systematically and the researcher needs to be explicit about how studies are singled out for description in a review and to be methodical when presenting detail of different studies. The synthesis is usually presented in the form of a structured narrative, summary tables or a statistical combination (meta-analysis) which is then used to formulate conclusions and recommendations. The EPPI-Centre 2007 model requires that the synthesis should be more than a listing of the results of individual studies and may take a variety of forms:

◆ *Statistical meta-analysis* – a set of statistical procedures designed to combine the numerical results of primary research studies addressing similar research questions.
◆ *Narrative empirical synthesis* – brings together the results of empirical research that are in a narrative form to provide an accessible combination of results from individual studies in structured narratives or summary tables.
◆ *Conceptual synthesis* – where different understandings or concepts about the World are brought together to create a new concept or concepts. For example, meta-ethnography combines the

results of different ethnographic studies to create an understanding of the phenomena under study, greater than the individual ethnographic studies.

(EPPI-Centre 2007, 2007e)

The systematic review model is undoubtedly becoming increasingly influential across the social sciences. Nonetheless, such an approach is not without its difficulties and remains contested, especially by positivist researchers who, quite rightly, have concerns that any research study that relies solely on such methods may merely compound and collate inadequacies of previous research studies. This is especially true in social research literature searches that, however systematic, may throw up articles and reports that are polemic in nature or the result of qualitative studies, such as ethnographic approaches, that may make no claim to generalisability. Nonetheless, it is also true that in social research one of the purposes of the literature review is to 'pay homage' to those that have gone before and whose work has been influential (Thody, 2006: 91) and the systematic approach will offer insurance that an analytical, thorough search has taken place even if the aims do not include the desire to complete a formal meta-analysis of previous outputs. Indeed many funding agencies expect or require a systematic study of the literature as a precursor to subsequent empirical study.

Making literature reviews more systematic

Whether or not the researcher decides to undertake a systematic review rather than a literature review the development of an orderly and methodical approach to searching for and, subsequently, examining the literature is a vital element in the likelihood of success in a research project. For this reason researchers should strive to make any exploration of the literature as systematic as possible. Figure 3.1 outlines a toolkit for making literature searches more systematic through a logical process of identifying key themes based on using research aims to inform research themes, leading to a rationale for database searches.

Once the relevant literature has been identified the researcher should adopt a critical approach to reading materials which will help them to focus their thoughts. The following points should be borne in mind:

◆ Skim the headings and the abstract of the piece, perhaps look at the first line of each paragraph and the conclusion.

Systematic Literature Review Toolkit (SLRT)

What is the overarching theme of the study?

Define four or five themes derived from research questions/issues/themes:

1.

2.

3.

4.

5.

Brainstorm five keywords for each of the themes to be explored:

1.	i.	ii.	iii	iv.	v.
2.	i.	ii.	iii.	iv.	v.
3.	i.	ii.	iii.	iv.	v.
4	i.	ii.	iii.	iv.	v.
5.	i.	ii.	iii.	iv.	v.

Note, the electronic databases to be explored:

1.   2.   3.

Outline the key areas to be explored in the review document for each item scrutinised, including:

Full reference with author/s, title, place of publication, edition, page numbers

Source (database)

Methodology employed by authors

Key themes

Key findings

Notes

List the key features that make your approach *systematic*:

Fig. 3.1 ◆ Systematic literature review toolkit

◆ Keep a critical focus. Who are the authors of this piece? What do you know about them?
◆ What is the perspective of the writer? (Think about the contexts of gender and culture.)
◆ Are the arguments logical?
◆ Is there reliable evidence to support the author's contentions?

(University of Melbourne, 2007b)

The extent to which this critical approach's questions are followed will help to determine the final quality of the written review. The problems of acquiring and storing material have been minimised in recent years since most journals are now held in digital format as well as hardcopy and, provided searches are carried out via an accredited University or other institutional search system, whole articles and documents can be downloaded from publisher's websites. Nonetheless, this mass of material itself presents challenges and the researcher should try to be systematic in the way that documents are stored. As simple system of creating folders and sub-folders that reflect the themes in searches, possibly allied to the actual key words entered, will enable speedy subsequent retrieval and obviate the need for much agonising when trying to locate 'lost' documents.

The systematic review process has as one of its elements the notion that a clear and consistent method of review for each retrieved item should be set up. The single researcher may decide to employ a wide range of alternative techniques such as simple note-taking but there is no reason why even the smallest of studies could employ a simple review document to record the seminal details of the items examined. Figure 3.2 provides a simple example of such a document.

Whether or not such a document is used the researcher should try to make connections between the project aims and the material being read and should compare and contrast the views of authors of the material as the 'narrative' of the research unfolds. In this way the researcher will be able to collate the mass of material that is available in order to formulate a conceptual map of the topic.

Using the literature review to develop a conceptual framework for a research study

The conceptual framework of a research study is that group of ideas, concepts and theoretical perspectives that give overall structure and coherence to a study.

Review document
Title:
Authors:
Full reference:
Methodology:
Key themes:
Key findings:
Notes:

Fig. 3.2 ◆ Literature review/systematic review document

In developing such a conceptual framework the researcher will draw on their original conception for the project, their discussions with colleagues, mentors, funding agency or supervisor, and the emerging ideas and previous research findings that derive from the literature. As outlined earlier, the aim of a literature review is to show that the writer has studied existing work in the field with insight and it is not enough merely to show what others in the field have discovered. In order to use this material as the basis of the conceptual framework the researcher will need to:

◆ compare and contrast different authors' views on an issue;
◆ group authors who draw similar conclusions;
◆ criticise aspects of methodology;
◆ note areas in which authors are in disagreement;
◆ highlight exemplary studies;
◆ highlight gaps in research;
◆ show how your study relates to previous studies;
◆ show how your study relates to the literature in general; and
◆ conclude by summarising what the literature says.

The idea of the literature review is to develop a good working knowledge of the research in a particular area. The final written review should reflect the results of this preliminary research. So, a good literature review raises questions and identifies areas to be explored (University of Melbourne, 2007a).

The resulting assessment of previous studies enables the researcher to explore their area of interest in considerable depth. The ideas, findings and theoretical perspectives that are the result of this process enable the researcher to refine and develop the conceptual framework for their research. This will be an iterative process since, as noted earlier, the initial research ideas and aims will serve to define the key themes and parameters in the literature survey, but the literature survey may serve to contradict previous conceptions and this may shut-off lines of enquiry or may open up entirely new areas of concern that need to be explored. This, the research questions or issues may themselves need to be adjusted or even altered considerably. This is a complex process since judgement is required about which new avenues of exploration may be valuable and relevant and there is always a danger that a study of the literature may open up whole new vistas of research that, although potentially fascinating, may actually lead the researcher away from their initial purposes, or may be so broad as to make the study untenable in terms of the time and resource available. The new researcher will find such issues especially problematic and consultation with a supervisor or research mentor may be invaluable at this point since experience will enable more practiced investigators to be able to judge which avenues of enquiry are likely to be productive and manageable which are not. The process of developing the conceptual framework is outlined in Fig. 3.3.

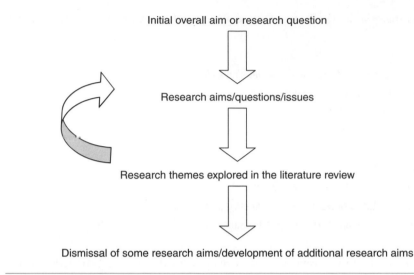

Initial overall aim or research question

Research aims/questions/issues

Research themes explored in the literature review

Dismissal of some research aims/development of additional research aims

Fig. 3.3 ◆ Development of conceptual framework

Some researchers take great care to frame their initial aims very carefully, whilst others leave initial aims, or issues more general and less concise with the deliberate intention that the final research aims will emerge as part of the literature review process. Such processes often reflect the methodological positions of the researcher, since positivist researchers tend to wish to define research questions very precisely from the outset with the intention of 'testing' the issues, whereas highly qualitative researchers frequently leave initial aims comparatively vague and avoid the use of terms like 'questions' altogether with the intention of allowing topics to reveal themselves in the process of research and writing.

Whichever approach the researcher chooses to take the most important factor is that the resultant set of ideas that are articulated and defended clearly so that the research funder, auditor or examiner can see very clearly the interconnecting theoretical structure that underpins the final research report and other outputs.

Conclusions

It is important to differentiate between a search, which is the process of accessing one or more manual or electronic databases or search engines, a literature review, which is an analytical summary of literature, and a systematic review, which employs many of the techniques of the review which enables researchers to conduct a meta-analysis of previous research and is recognised increasingly as a methodology in its own right. Almost all studies will require one or more databases searches, even if only to confirm that comparatively little literature has been generated on a topic in the past; most serious studies undertaken as part of postgraduate study or during funded research, will require a number of structured searches against a clearly identified set of criteria. The subsequent analysis of the material elicited from such searches, whether in the form of a traditional or more systematic review, will inform the subsequent research process and help to inform the conceptual framework for the study.

An initial exposition of this conceptual framework should underpin the introductory statement of a research report or thesis, even if the term is not employed at that stage. This underpinning theoretical construction should then be subject to further clarification during the analysis of previous research embodied in the literature review and should be exemplified in the discussion, analysis and conclusions of the study. The processes whereby this exemplification takes place may be both overt and subtle. For instance, the researcher may provide clear and signposted statements of the theoretical or methodological 'position' that they intend to take and how this relates to a particular intellectual tradition. Such statements will usually come early in the study and scaffold the later analytical framework. Later on it is unlikely that there will be room for such direct exposition but the conceptual framework will guide the direction of the study and will be revealed by reference back to key literature explored earlier, comparison with previous research findings, and through the general line of argument presented by the researcher.

FURTHER READING

◆ Bell, J., *Doing your Research Project* (4th Ed) Buckingham: Open University Press (2005)

◆ Blaxter, L., Hughes, C. and Tight, M., *How to Research*, Buckingham: Open University Press (1996)

◆ Edwards, A. ad Talbot, R., *The Hard-Pressed Researcher: A Research Handbook for the Caring Professions*, London: Addison Wesley Longman (1999)

◆ Oliver, S. and Peersman, G. (Eds) *Using Research for Effective Health Promotion*, Buckingham: Open University Press (2001)

◆ Potter, S., *Doing Postgraduate Research*, London: Sage (2002)

◆ Gough, D., 'Systematic research synthesis to inform the development of policy and practice in education', in Thomas, G. and Pring, R. (Eds) *Evidence-based Practice*, Buckingham: Open University Press, pp 44–62 (2004)

Section 2
Planning and Preparation

Once the purpose of the research has been established, the focus then moves on to the consideration of who will be best placed to provide you with the information that you seek – your research population. Frequently there are simply too many in this population for you to ask them all so you will require guidance on how you can select from the population to make your research more manageable. The consideration of how you can most effectively ask your research population for the information that you require is important, that said, the majority of section 2 consists of advice on how to help you make the best choices for your particular situation, on an appropriate approach for your research and the most effective methodologies to support it.

Who To Ask

This chapter will focus on the following learning outcomes, each of which relates to a specific aspect to be considered in the selection of research participants and/or other data sources. By the time you have read this chapter you should be able, for your chosen research focus to:

◆ identify potential respondents to form a research population;
◆ appreciate the need to justify the choice of respondents;
◆ understand the purpose of sampling from a larger population and justify the sampling method; and
◆ demonstrate a critical awareness of potential ethical issues that need to be addressed.

Introduction

In our consideration of possible research topics we are usually guided by a personal or professional interest, issues and problems of which we have become aware and wish to investigate further. For example, as a teacher you may have become increasingly aware of inconsistencies in pupil behaviour, which you attribute to factors inherent in the classroom environment. In order to explore your ideas more systematically you would like to conduct a research study. This could involve a survey covering a large number of schools within your region or follow a case study approach based on your own school. A third option might be action research with a much narrower focus on your own pupils and possibly in collaboration with other colleagues. It goes without saying that in order to plan your research you need to identify the population with which your study will be concerned. Will it include all pupils in the school or a specific age or ability group, or only those displaying unpredictable and inconsistent behaviour patterns?

Once you have established the population you may find that for practical reasons (for example, cost, time, accessibility) you need to base your investigation on a smaller group or a sub-set of the total population originally identified. This is where you have to ask yourself a series of pertinent questions:

1. What is the purpose of the research? Is it about generalisable outcomes or gaining a deeper understanding of the educational process to inform practice in a specific setting?
2. How will I gain access to the research participants? Who are the gatekeepers from whom I need to seek permission to enter the field? Headteacher or colleagues?
3. What are the logistical challenges that need to be overcome (for example, travel, time, administrative duties, etc)?
4. What are the potential ethical issues to be considered, such as seeking informed consent from adults, vulnerable groups or children?

Selecting a sample

As the primary concern of practitioner research is generally considered to be the improvement of professional practice, it normally precludes large scale surveys for the generation of generalisable outcomes. Instead, samples are relatively small, but nevertheless have to be selected carefully from a total population. Population in this respect does not exclusively denote people, but is to be understood as 'the total number of possible units or elements that are included in the study' or 'the totality of people, organisations, objects or occurrences from which a sample is drawn' (Gray, 2004: 82; 403). This can, for example, include the selection of venues, times and type of data sources. Selecting your sample appropriately is, therefore, key, particularly where there is no research funding, and minimal or no administrative support available. First, you need to familiarise yourself with a range of sampling methods to enable you to make an informed decision on their appropriateness for your investigation. The research literature distinguishes between two major categories: probability or representative sampling, used in surveys with the intention to produce generalisable outcomes in the form of statistical inferences, and non-probability samples, usually employed in small-scale studies, such as practitioner research.

Probability sampling

In probability sampling the sample must be representative of the population from which it was drawn. As such it must share the same characteristics. If a population is sufficiently homogenous *random sampling* can be applied, in that each member of the population has a chance of being selected. For example, a headteacher may wish to canvass the views of parents'/carers' on homework policy. Given that the pupils enrolled at the school display a highly diverse population in terms of gender, ability, socio-economic status, ethnicity, religion and culture, the challenge is how to ensure that the results of the survey are representative in relation to all the identified sub-groups. While some of those groups may be rather homogeneous in their behaviour, others may display highly diverse characteristics. In this case *stratified sampling* may be appropriate, as it reflects the proportion of the various sub-groups involved and thus prevents skewing of the data in favour of a group that is actively engaged with the process, as opposed to one where only a minority of group members responded. Another frequently asked question is that of sample size. However, there is no hard and fast rule. As a general guideline, Cohen *et al* (2007) state 30 as a minimum for statistical analysis.

Non-probability sampling

As most practitioner research is conducted in the researcher's own practice setting, it will involve relatively small, non-probability samples and be predominantly of a qualitative nature. Nevertheless, samples and sampling methods have to be selected with care, always bearing in mind the purpose of the investigation and potential logistical, methodological, epistemological and ethical issues. The most commonly employed non-probability sampling methods are:

◆ *Purposive sampling* – researcher uses his/her own judgement in the selection of participants in relation to certain characteristics or traits. For example, a study investigating the perceived crisis in modern foreign languages (MFLs) could include all those pupils who have decided against continuing their studies beyond KS4.
◆ *Quota sampling* – similar to stratified sampling it contains sub-groups of the total population in the proportion in which they occur in the particular research setting. Returning to the example above, a quota sample could take into account distribution of gender, ability, ethnic background and socio-economic status of Year 11 pupils within a school.
◆ *Convenience or volunteer sampling* – by taking advantage of personal or professional contacts and relationships researchers choose individuals who are relatively easy to reach. According to Robson (2002: 265) 'it is probably one of the most widely used and least satisfactory methods of sampling' and, heeding the caveat supplied by Gray, 'needs to be treated with extreme caution' (2004: 88), as the representativeness of the sample cannot be determined. For example, sixth

formers are invited to provide monthly feedback on the any aspects of their learning environment (for example, quality of teaching, learning environment, assessment, guidance and support systems, social events, etc). However, there is no way of ascertaining how representative the comments are of the total student body. What about those who do not reply?

◆ *Snowball sampling* as the term implies, this sampling method starts with a small number of individuals who have been selected by the researcher on the basis of specific characteristics relevant to the study and who can identify other individuals potentially eligible for inclusion in the research. Often this method is employed when it is difficult to identify suitable participants or where highly sensitive topics can raise the issue of intrusion of privacy, emotional upset and loss of dignity. Examples relating to this category would include investigations into drug abuse, eating disorder, sexual behaviour or bullying.

In helping you select the appropriate sample type it is useful to consider the following aspects:

◆ ease of access to the research setting and research participants (viz. negotiation with gatekeepers);
◆ the number of perspectives to be represented in relation to the research focus (for example, teachers, parents/carers, pupils, support staff, managers);
◆ the researcher's positionality in relation to the research setting and participants, particularly critical in insider research (the balance of power between researcher and researched);
◆ the participant's competence to give informed consent to participate (ethics guidelines);
◆ legal requirements, for example, with regard to the involvement of children in research;
◆ logistical challenges, for example, travel, interview venue availability; and
◆ funding of data collection (postal distribution of questionnaires).

Gaining access

There are two, more likely three, levels of access to be negotiated before any evidence is gathered in order to assure the ethical standards of the proposed research are adequate – the British Educational Research Association (BERA) (www.bera.ac.uk) provide guidance for the researcher in this respect. The first is the need to confirm that the gatekeeper of your proposed research population (if one can be identified) is in agreement with your research aims and the tools that you intend to use – the headteacher of the school, for example. If you are working towards an academic qualification you will also need to satisfy the ethical requirements of the organisation you are studying with. Finally you will need to explain the purpose of your research to your potential respondents so that they are:

◆ fully informed of the reasons for the data collection;
◆ assure them that responses will be held in confidence (and ultimately, securely destroyed);
◆ assure them that their anonymity will be maintained where their responses might be reported in any published form; (the purpose of any identifier placed on any questionnaire or test will need to be explained); and
◆ informed that they have the option not to participate.

This may be communicated as part of a covering letter or verbal introduction to the data collection. Cohen *et al* (2007: 339) provide a fairly definitive list of what should be included in such letters.

The gatekeeper

In the complex mechanism of bureaucratic, technical and logistical difficulties, gate-keepers and key informants play a crucial role in the process of gaining access, with issues of building trusts and developing relationships lying at the heart of the process. As much as they can hamper the process of data collection, they can equally well function as 'catalysts' in the process of reaching compromises, taking short-cuts … bringing about serendipitous occurrences (Walford, 1987: 1), which can enhance the quality and quantity of data collected.

As a teacher you may consider your 'insider' position as a distinct advantage. This is often based on the assumption that access is automatically granted and pupils and/or colleagues are only too willing to participate in your study. However, before you start approaching any potential research participants you need to obtain the gatekeeper's permission to proceed. Particularly where the research outcomes may have an impact on part of, or the whole school, it is not only courteous but is also considered good research practice to consult the headteacher and any other colleagues whose department may be affected by your study. It will also allay any potential concerns and anxieties and adhere to the ethical principle of informed consent. In providing information about your research to gatekeepers you may need to include the following key points:

◆ background to the project in terms of the local, regional or national context;
◆ purpose of the research, including key objectives;

◆ definition of the group of participants and procedures involved;
◆ phases of the research;
◆ audience to whom the research outcomes may be of interest or benefit; and
◆ contact details for further information.

In seeking gatekeepers' permission to proceed with the research it is vital to provide clear and detailed information about the purpose of the research, the participants and relevant procedures. Where a cluster of schools is involved, as might be the case in an evaluative study concerned with the social inclusion of children with SEN in mainstream education, it would be appropriate to seek the Local Authority's (LAs) approval. As Measor and Woods (1984) highlighted in their study in a comprehensive school, any shortcuts taken at this stage may result in blockage at a later stage of the research process, which manifested itself in the breakdown of relationships and trust between the research and gatekeepers and ultimately the end of the investigation. Gaining access to the research setting is thus closely linked to establishing trust-based relationships with gatekeepers and key informants.

Ethical issues

Teachers and researchers share one common responsibility, namely 'duty of care' in relation to all those participating in the research process. Behaving in an ethical manner will also increase the chances of maintaining positive relationships between researcher and research participants for the duration of the study. As Groundwater and Mockler comment: 'quality action (and practitioner) research is in its very nature an ethical business' (2007: 209). By locating the enquiry within their own practice context and professional experience, practitioner action researchers distinguish themselves from traditional researchers by: 'their interdependence of the activities of university academics and educators in particular' (Kemmis & McTaggart, 2000: 567).

Given that practitioner research is conducted by teachers already located within the research setting, gaining access does not pose any great challenges. In fact, classroom practitioners may have difficulty distinguishing between data collection they undertake as a classroom practitioner with the aim of reviewing, analysing and improving teaching and learning processes and similar activities commonly associated with practice-based research. For example, information gathered via pupil observation, a questionnaire survey involving parents/carers or face-to-face interviews with colleagues may be used internally to inform and improve professional practice, but, equally, could be made available in the public domain to a much wider audience. In this case, we would view the process as being more akin to research rather than merely constituting an aspect of professional practice. It would require careful exploration of the potential ethical issues inherent in the research setting and the selection of strategies which address them appropriately. 'Insider' research can thus be problematic and raise issues of the balance of power, ownership and voice, anonymity and confidentiality and informed consent, to which we will return later in greater detail.

Ethics have always been recognised as a central element in medical and scientific research, but during the past ten years or so, there has been a growing awareness of ethical issues in relation to practitioner research in educational settings, particularly action research. In view of the increase of practitioner research at postgraduate and doctoral level, higher education institutions (HEIs) increasingly require students to apply for ethical approval prior to commencing their investigation and to comply with a set of prescribed procedures and principles as set out in the university's ethics code. A particularly useful source of information on ethical issues is the *Revised Ethical Guidelines for Educational Research* (2004) published by the BERA. It is unambiguous, easily accessible and provides a useful reference point for practitioners intending to conduct research in their professional practice setting. Nevertheless, the distinction between an ethical, moral and legally defensible approach is not always clear cut, as all three are concerned with the protection of individuals: physically, psychologically, emotionally or in any other conceivable form. For example, the introduction of a new strategy designed to assist pupils in developing their reading skills is to be evaluated. To ensure the quality of the research, one group of pupils will be exposed to the new strategy, while a control group does not have the opportunity of enjoying the potential benefits of this innovative intervention. Whilst such procedure is perfectly legal, it raises ethical issues of fairness and inclusion. Similarly, deliberately misleading a group of participants, for example, to test their resilience to powerful means of persuasion in the safe knowledge that no one will come to any harm, is predominantly a moral issue. In contrast, the observation and video recording of children's behaviour in the playground would first and foremost constitute a legal issue, although as part of their professional role teachers regularly observe and record pupils' behaviour. What is at issue here is the future use of the material, that is, whether it will be available in the public domain.

In essence, the aims of an ethical approach to research involving human beings is to develop and maintain non-exploitative social and personal relationships, and to enhance the social and emotional lives of those who participate (Stringer, 1999).

For education practitioners who intend to conduct research in their own or other colleagues' institutions the following list of guidelines may be helpful and should be considered prior to starting the research:

1. All research participants need to have a full understanding of the research purpose, the activities in which they will be involved (for example, time, venue, additional disruption to daily routine), any potential risks involved and what will happen to the data in terms with regard to publication.
2. Participation must be entirely voluntary. Incentives to participate (for example, raffle, prize draw, vouchers) should be kept within reasonable limits.
3. Participants must be made aware of the right to withdraw at any stage of the research without any negative consequences or incurring loss of services received.
4. Informed consent must be obtained from all those participating in the investigation and where this involves vulnerable groups and children, it includes their guardians, such as parents, carers and/or teachers.
5. Any intrusion of the participants' privacy must be avoided.
6. Additional stress, such as investigating sensitive issues requiring participants to spend time in addition to their normal work schedule must be kept to a minimum.
7. All information divulged by the research participants must be stored securely.
8. Unless agreed otherwise, any records, such as audio/video recordings and transcripts must be destroyed following completion of the research.
9. Anonymity of participants and confidentiality of information must be assured.
10. There must never be any coercion on participants to behave in a certain way.

Ownership

To ensure a sense of inclusion and ownership amongst all stakeholders it is vital that all their perspectives are considered in the design of the action and its implementation. This presents challenges to the person leading the project in terms of providing effective leadership and in managing potential ethical issues. We would now like you to consider Scenario 4.1, which raises potential issues and poses pertinent questions of how they should be addressed.

Scenario 4.1

Within the agenda of raising achievement as well as *Every Child Matters*, a school's senior management team has identified issues with regard to pupil transition from KS2 to KS3. To assist pupils in managing transition it was decided to implement a new curriculum for Year 7 pupils, which will mirror some of the conditions prevailing in a primary education setting.

Year 7 teachers will be attached to a mixed ability class in a designated classroom, teaching across a range of subjects. It is hoped that within a stable learning environment and through regular contact with their teacher and peers, pupils in 'their own base' will be helped to form positive relationships, develop a sense of cohort identity and belonging and, as a consequence, will be better equipped to manage the challenges of transfer from primary to secondary school and from KS2 to KS3. The aim of this intervention is to enhance the quality of pupils' learning experiences, to generate a sense of well being and ultimately to raise achievement.

However, the response from school staff is divided. While some teachers are excited at the prospect of stepping outside the boundaries of their subject specialism, others are very unhappy at the prospect of having to confine their teaching almost exclusively to Year 7 and of losing the intellectual stimulation of working with older GCSE and AS/A level students. Furthermore, they expressed concern about having to teach subjects in which they lack knowledge and expertise.

An assistant headteacher, who is aspiring to take on a headship in their foreseeable future, and who is currently selecting a topic for a MA dissertation in Education and Management, would like to take this opportunity for conducting an action research project as part of the dissertation.

Points to consider:

- the composition of the research team to ensure ownership across stakeholders;
- the kind of data that should be collected;
- inclusion of a range of perspectives via triangulation;
- potential ethical issues arising from insider action research; and
- seeking consent.

Balance of power

Conducting action research in your own institution can lull you into a false sense of security, as you are familiar with the setting and know the actors within it. Insiders often have knowledge not only about an institution but also about the people who work within it and those who are designated to participate in the action research (Costley & Gibbs, 2006). The combination of these factors may engender ambivalent feelings towards you amongst your colleagues. In your role as researcher, you may suddenly be perceived in a different light, namely as someone who has a hidden agenda and can, therefore, not be trusted unconditionally. In addition, you may occupy a position of power within your institution's management system, inadvertently affecting colleagues' behaviour towards you in a number of ways. There may be a faction within your school who perceive the research exercise as a fortuitous opportunity to promote their own interests and air their personal or departmental grievances in the hope that they can influence the outcome of the research and thus have an impact on strategic decisions relevant to them. Others may want to demonstrate their loyalty to you by giving you the responses which they believe you expect, while some may feel intimidated and will be less likely to share their views with you in an honest manner. As in teaching, the appropriate use of language is, therefore, critical. For instance, referring to participants as 'subjects' would not only be wholly inappropriate from a professional point of view, but be incompatible with the democratic principles inherent in the philosophy underpinning practitioner research. Particularly within an action research context, the notions of inclusion and ownership are central and the representation of marginalised and vulnerable groups is one of the core aims.

If the research involves children, the issue of balance of power can be even more pronounced. By asking them to complete a questionnaire or take part in an interview, there is the danger that they do not perceive the researcher in you, but the teacher, and that instead of 'honest', they may feel that they have to give 'right' answers, which would impair the validity of their responses. Similar issues may arise in undertaking focus group discussion involving a mix of pupils, some of whom have established themselves as leaders who voice their opinions openly and vociferously, whilst others, under the influence of peer pressure, lack the confidence to do so. As a consequence the data gathered will reflect a certain bias in favour of a certain group of pupils. How can you, as their teacher, ensure that the focus group allows all pupils to express their views without restriction and thus minimise the potential of bias in favour of a dominant group?

Scenario 4.2 – Focus group discussion involving Year 9 pupils

A male tutor would like to investigate the incidence of bullying amongst 34 Year 9 pupils. This is the composition of his form:

	Boys 19				
	British born 17			**Born outside UK** 2	
White	Asian Muslim	African Caribbean	Polish	Asian Muslim	African Caribbean
11	4	2	1	1	0

	Girls 15				
	British born 14			**Born outside UK** 1	
White	Asian Muslim	African Caribbean	Polish	Asian Muslim	African Caribbean
7	6	1	0	1	0

Points to consider:

- appropriate group size;
- composition of the group;
- suitability of venue;
- length of conversation; and
- recording of data.

Whilst these issues are of an ethical nature in relation to the balance of power and control, they can also have serious epistemological and methodological implications in terms of the way in which they affect the quantity and quality of data generated and introduce bias in the construction of knowledge. Furthermore, ethical issues, such as protection of participants' identity and confidentiality of information divulged, are of utmost importance with regard to the dissemination of findings in the public domain. The strict adherence to ethical guidelines, which stipulate voluntary participation, informed consent and the right to withdraw from the research without suffering any negative consequences as the key aspects to consider are, therefore, paramount. Useful information in relation to these issues is provided in *Revised Ethical Guidelines for Educational Research* (BERA, 2004).

Informed consent

One issue which is problematic for practitioner researcher, particularly where children are involved, is that of 'informed consent' and voluntary participation, including the right to withdrawal at any stage of the research. First of all, it has to be established who is giving consent for what. Consider the scenario below in relation to the issue of 'informed consent':

Scenario 4.3

A primary headteacher is planning an intervention involving a health and fitness programme, specifically aimed at children at risk of becoming clinically obese. The intervention is delivered by staff from the local university and consists of a dietary plan and a physical activity schedule for a whole term.

Key points to consider:

- timing of the intervention – as part of school curriculum during or in addition/instead of nature of research topic;
- assuring protection of participants' identity and confidentiality of divulged information;
- seeking informed consent – parents'/carers', teachers', children's;
- participants' level of competence to access the information provided;
- identification of potential social, cultural, linguistic barriers; and
- participants' right to withdraw.

In order to ensure that the information given is fully understood by all participants, it may be necessary to produce a customised participant information sheet for each sub-group of the entire sample, which takes account of their specific characteristics and needs in terms of the way in which the information is presented. This may involve appropriate use of language, clear layout and larger than usual font size as illustrated. It may also include a specific colour scheme, for example, blue script on yellow background, to cater for the needs of dyslexia and colour blindness.

As in the production of participant information sheets, a differentiated approach needs to be taken with regard to seeking consent. Participants' consent may be implicit by return of self-completion, but will have to be sought explicitly in the case of interviews, focus groups, interventions, etc. The question of whether you always need to obtain parents'/carers' consent is not easy to answer, as the literature provides a range of perspectives on this issue. For example, the *Revised Ethical Guidelines for Educational Research* (BERA, 2004: 7) state that: 'in the case of participants whose age, intellectual ability or other vulnerable circumstance may limit the extent to which they can be expected to undertake their role, researchers must [...] seek the collaboration and approval of those who act in guardianship (for example, parents) or as 'responsible others' (BERA, 2004: 7). This introduces further considerations in relation to the participants' competence, which may be determined by their age, intellectual ability, level of emotional maturity and their social and cultural background. Masson (2004) defends the view that a social researcher who does not seek parents'/carers' consent for an under 16-year-old participant should not be at risk of legal procedures brought by parents/carers, unless it is about causing harm to the child. According to Fine and Sandstrom (1988) it is the nature of the research that is critical. They believe that the headteacher's consent is sufficient unless the children are involved in an extreme form of research. Sieber (1992) goes as far as to maintain that parental permission may be waived when it is difficult to locate parents/carers and when the research will have no adverse effect on the children involved. In a similar vein, Hill promotes the argument that, where a child has the capacity to decide about participation there is no need for parental permission' (Hill, 2005: 70). Lindsay (2000) argues that where information is not released on any individual child, consent may be obtained from the school rather than the parent.

Given that the law relates to the notion of 'competence' (See Masson, 2002; Anderson & Morrow, 2004), it seems reasonable to suggest that parent/carer consent can be waived where a child can be judged to 'understand' what participation in a particular project will involve. In such circumstances it is questionable whether a parent/carer has the right to override the child's wishes. The United Nations Conventions of the Rights of the Child states that: 'all actions concerning the children must be in their best interest' (Art. 3). 'Children who are capable of forming their own views should be granted the right to express their own views freely [...] children should therefore be facilitated to give fully informed consent' (Art. 12).

Conclusion

Having considered a wide range of issues in relation to sampling, gaining access and informed consent, we should take heed of the caveat presented by Stanley and Sieber (1995), who remind us that not everything that is legal is 'ethical' and that: 'ethics has to do with the application of moral principles to prevent harming or wronging others, to promote the good, to be respectful and to be fair' (Sieber, 1993: 14). As in teaching, there is a strong pragmatic dimension inherent in practitioner research, requiring the researcher to display attributes commonly associated with Schön's (1983) concept of 'reflective practice,' and a professional and moral responsibility to those in their care.

FURTHER READING

◆ British Education Research Association (BERA) *Revised Ethical Guidelines for Educational Research*, Southwell, BERA (2004)

◆ Cohen, L., Manion, L. and Morrison, K., *Research Methods in Education* (6th Ed) Abingdon: Routledge (2007)

◆ Gray, D. E., *Doing research in the real world*, London: Sage (2004)

◆ Hill, M., 'Ethical considerations in researching children's experiences', in S. Greene and D. Hogan, (Eds) *Researching children's experiences: approaches and methods*, London: Sage, 61–86 (2005)

◆ Robson, C., *Real world research* (2nd Ed) Oxford: Blackwell (2002)

 # How To Ask – Decisions, Decisions!

By the conclusion of this chapter it is anticipated that you will:

◆ be aware of different approaches to research;
◆ be able to match the approach to the context and research aims; and
◆ appreciate the need to justify the model, approach and method adopted.

Section 1 of this book broadly focused on 'what to ask'. By analysing the context you are able to focus on the 'key issues' that will form the basis of your study. Through a thorough exploration of the literature you will have become aware of alternative theories and the outcomes of past research performed in this field. From these twined beginnings you will have established the key questions that must be maintained at the heart of your research if it is to maintain consistency and rigour. In the previous chapter we have concentrated on the identification of the likely key respondents – those who are best placed to provide you with the information that you need to be able to address your key research questions, and how to decide on the number of potential respondents (sampling). This last point, sampling of your population, is also driven by the nature of your evidence gathering technique – the appropriateness of some methods is closely related to the size of the sample. For example, a survey by self-completion questionnaire is most likely to be administered to a large sample, while interviews are usually conducted with smaller numbers of respondents.

Models of research – a philosophical starting point

If it is possible to draw a line between 'researchers' and 'practitioners' (who 'dabble' in research activity), then this is where it is probably drawn. All professions, to a greater or lesser extent, become 'precious' of their terminology to a point where communication of key ideas with 'lay people' becomes problematic. In chapter 1, some of this terminology was hinted at. Whilst it is the intention to explore the terminology in greater depth here, it still must be regarded as a highly superficial encounter.

Whilst there are a growing number of models of inquiry (*paradigms*), here we will focus on the two most frequently associated with educational research; the so-called positivistic/scientific and the interpretive paradigm. With this in mind we have attempted to construct a simplified diagram (Table 5.1) to provide an overview of the key concepts and terminology associated with each paradigm.

For centuries, positivism has been the prevailing paradigm, while interpretivism has established itself relatively late as an alternative, challenging traditional assumptions underpinning research. Both paradigms represent opposing worldviews with regard to the way in which reality is understood (ontology) and the production of knowledge (epistemology) is perceived. Reality is believed to be objective and external to the observer. Accordingly 'the purpose of research is to develop … confidence that a particular knowledge claim … is true or false by collecting evidence in the form of objective data of relevant phenomena' (Mewrtens & McClaughlin, 2004:52).

A positivistic researcher seeks generalisations and 'hard' quantitative, measurable data by means of employing a scientific approach.

In contrast, an interpretive researcher aims to explore perspectives and shared meanings and to develop insights and a deeper understanding of phenomena occurring in the social world by means of collecting predominantly qualitative data. Reality is perceived as human construct.

In relation to the two paradigms, further distinction can be drawn between a naturalistic and an experimental approach. While the former is conducted in a natural setting, the latter takes place under controlled conditions (clinical laboratory, control groups).

However, we need to include a caveat here, as the distinction between these two paradigms can be rather simplistic. Although certain research approaches and methods tend to reside in either the positivistic or the interpretive paradigm, there is overlap in the way in which methods are used within specific paradigms. Indeed, a mixed methodology is often adopted, combining qualitative with quantitative data. Whilst an interpretive investigator will doubt whether a scientific/positivistic approach can adequately explore and explain human behaviour, a scientific/positivistic researcher will collect data which are of generalisable value. The probability of an event will be calculated as a precise numerical value, that is, its statistical significance. Consequently, each approach has its strengths and weaknesses and its appropriateness depends on the nature of the enquiry and the type of information that is required.

To enable you to distinguish clearly between an interpretive and positivistic framework it is important that you understand the philosophical principles underpinning and the methodological preferences generally associated with each of these two paradigms. With the intention of making the differences and potential overlap between the two paradigms apparent, we have devised a number of questions and provided answers in relation to each paradigm (Table 5.1).

Table 5.1 ◆ Competing research paradigms

Interpretive		Positivist
Reality is a construct. It is multi-dimensional and ever changing and is dependent on different frames of reference.	1. How is reality defined? **(Ontology)**	Reality is to be discovered. It is objective, rational and independent from the observer.
The research process is underpinned by democratic principles, giving equal status to participants and welcoming diversity of perspectives. The researcher forms part of the research setting and is affected by it (for example, insider/outsider position). Issues related to status, power, ownership and control (gender, race, class, culture, political perspective) are important.	2. How does the researcher perceive him/herself in relation to the research setting? **(Positionality)**	The researcher is objective and independent from the research setting/ experiment (outsider position). Negation of self, as personal values impair the scientist's objectivity/impartiality. The researcher operates within clearly defined parameters, following pre-determined procedures. Observation is viewed as uncontaminated.
Qualitative data, but not exclusively. Insights, deeper knowledge and understanding of human behaviour and relationship. Exploring different perspectives relating to one phenomenon. Uniqueness.	3. What is (are) the purpose/aim(s) of the research? **(Rationale)**	Qualitative data. Generalisations. Proving/disproving of hypothesis. Searching for the 'truth'. Hypotheses are derived from theories and are submitted to empirical tests for verification and rejection.

Continued

Table 5.1 ◆ *Cont'd*

Interpretive		Positivist
The construction of knowledge is a democratic process, involving both researcher and research participants. Knowledge is constructed from multiple perspectives. The element of subjectivity and bias is acknowledged and declared – the 'belief' system underpinning the viewpoint of the research (for example, feminist research).	4. How is knowledge created? **(Epistemology)**	The researcher is perceived as the 'guardian' and 'creator of knowledge' and as such occupies a position of authority in relation to the research 'subjects'. Only those phenomena that are observable and measurable can validly be warranted as knowledge (empiricism).
Theory building is perceived as an ever-developing entity, not a perfect product. It is central to the research process and emerges from the dialogue between theoretical and professional perspectives and the data gathered (for example, grounded theory). The conceptual framework around which the research is constructed emerges gradually (inductive method).	5. What role does theory play?	Theory and hypothesis testing provide the rationale for the research and inform its design. The conceptual framework underpinning the research design is pre-determined (deductive method).
Credibility and trustworthiness (building confidence in the accuracy of the data); internal validity (thick description, rich, dense data through triangulation); and transferability, relatability, translatability of findings across similar settings.	6. What are the quality criteria of 'good' research?	External validity (the data are accurate and are also valid in relation to other contexts); reliability (concerned with the consistency of measure); generalisability (the research results also apply to other settings); and statistical significance.
Voluntary participation based on informed consent; anonymity of participants and confidentiality of information divulged; protection of research participants against potentially harmful consequences; protection of privacy; and giving voice and ownership to the research participants.	7. What ethical issues need to be considered?	Voluntary participation based on informed consent; anonymity of participants and confidentiality of information divulged; protection of research participants against harmful; and consequences (risk assessment).

Finally, to help you distinguish between the purpose for adopting a quantitative or a qualitative methodology, it is useful to refer to the metaphors applied by Kvale (1996).

Accordingly the qualitative researcher can be perceived as a:

> 'traveller on a journey that leads to a tale to be told upon returning home. The (researcher)-traveller wanders through the landscape and enters into conversations with people encountered. The traveller explores the many domains of the country, as unknown territory and with maps, roaming freely around the territory' (Kvale, 1996:4)

In contrast, quantitative research can be likened to the process of mining. In this metaphor: 'knowledge is understood as buried metal and the researcher is a miner who unearths the valuable metal ... the knowledge is waiting in the subject's interior to be uncovered, uncontaminated by the miner' (Kvale, 1996:3). Taber (2007:34) helpfully refers to positivism and interpretism as ERP1 and ERP2 (educational research paradigm). In the same way that it is useful to be aware, as a teacher, for example, that you are employing a 'positive behaviour management' approach to control a class, as this awareness should also allow you to make direct links to complementary techniques; similarly, awareness of research paradigms, in respect of what you hope to achieve, will provide an indication of the evidence gathering techniques that are most likely to be appropriate and effective.

Worked Example 1

You wish to explore the development of speaking and listening skills within a nursery setting.

The use of predetermined criteria (developed from a published theory, model or research findings) would imply a positivist standpoint and suggest a choice from a particular range of approaches (focusing mainly on the need to collect and collate data of a comparative nature). Previous research will inform the ontology.

Entering the nursery setting with a more 'open' perspective would mean that all information being presented is, potentially, of equal importance and it is the role of the researcher to select

Continued

and record appropriately. This is where epistemological issues about how and what kind of knowledge is produced have to be considered. The perspective of the researcher will inevitably influence the selection data collected and 'edit' the information to be retained and organised. For example, will the researcher focus on resource and organisational aspects which appear to impact upon the children's development or place more emphasis on the quality of social interactions between the children or children and adults? Will the information to be gathered consist of measurable 'hard' (quantitative) data generated through standardised testing or will it be made up of 'soft' (qualitative) data, reflecting the participants' feelings, experiences and opinions?

Approaches to research

In research literature there is wide range of terminology employed to describe paradigms, approaches, methodologies, strategies, techniques, methods, instruments and tools – all of which can be rather confusing to the practitioner researcher. Similarly in teaching, the use of acronyms and jargon is not always understood by pupils and parents and those outside the profession. Whilst Denscombe (2003) distinguishes between a number of alternative research strategies, Cohen *et al* (2007) list different 'styles', while Walliman (2003) prefers to use 'types' and Bell (2005) 'approaches' – lists with similar, but by no means identical content.

Interestingly, both Cohen *et al* (2007) and Denscombe (2003) list 'Internet-based research' at this organisational level (alongside ethnography, case studies and action research), but it might also be argued that this is simply the technology by which the researcher gains access to the research population (or published information) – there are no similar sections for 'telephone' or 'library', for example. Walliman's inclusion of feminist and cultural approaches perhaps could be construed as being particular perspectives from which to perform ethnographic research.

Cohen *et al* (2007) then continue by examining various evidence gathering *strategies* – which Bell (2005), Walliman (2003) and Denscombe (2003) refer to as *methods*, a further confusion of terminology which can be found when comparing almost any two texts written on educational research. Here we will use 'methods'. The structure given in Fig. 5.1 may help to clarify some of the terms used. Particular approaches complement the paradigms through the nature of the evidence that is related to the

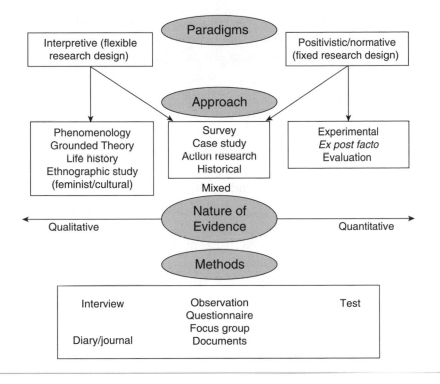

Fig. 5.1 ◆ Research terminology

methods. A case study, for example, may be adopted via either paradigm, however, the nature of the evidence and the actual methodology will reflect the philosophy underpinning the chosen paradigm (qualitative or quantitative) for the research activity.

The examples given in Table 5.1 will also help you to distinguish between an overall methodology and specific methods residing within it. Thus the adoption of a research perspective should be considered of a higher order than the selection of a research approach/strategy and be considered to inform that selection.

Grounded theory, developed by Glaser and Strauss (1967), is a pragmatic approach to the development of theories which are useful to those working 'on the ground' (Locke, 2001: 59). However, the term 'grounded' refers to the development of theory from the data, thus grounding the emergent theory in the data. At the same time it must be acknowledged that theory does not immediately spring from the data but is subject, according to Hayes (2000:184) to 'a cyclical process in which theoretical insights emerge'. In other words, the process of data collection and analysis will involve a dialogical relationship between the data and existing (literature, professional knowledge and experience) and emerging concepts.

In this sense it is firmly located within the interpretive paradigm. In its purest form, a grounded theory approach requires the researcher to enter the research setting without holding any preconceptions or socio-cultural/political biases. However, practitioner research is usually provoked by a speculation, an issue or a problem that has arisen within the context of professional practice and may also be informed by government frameworks, policy and literature.

Action research also relies upon a cyclical process which is iterative in nature. The aim is usually to bring about some desired change over a period of time which involves a series of interventions by the researcher(s), each one being informed by an analysis of the impact of the previous one and, as such, is possibly the most familiar to teachers, as it closely resembles the *plan-teach-assess/evaluate-plan* cycle. The approach will be explored in much greater detail in chapter 9. The aim of action research is thus not primarily to generate knowledge but to improve professional practice within a democratic context of collaboration and inclusion.

The *experimental* approach is worth examining not least because of the concerns that it throws up when attempting to gain ethical approval for a piece of research! As with scientific experiments, a variable is changed and the effect is gauged, judged or measured by comparison with a control group. The concern revolves around the concept of 'harm' that can be caused to the research participants, either by being subjected to the variable or by not having access to it – a particular learning resource or strategy, for example. An allied approach which is less intrusive and problematic, from the perspective of the researcher at least, is ex post facto. This involves a retrospective analysis of the impact of a change or specific factor – the improvements in reading in Year 2 classes that have been using a particular reading strategy over the past year against those that haven't (assuming allowances for any other factors).

According to Bogdan and Biklen (1982, cited in Wellington, 2000:38), 'a case study is a detailed examination of one or more settings, or a single subject, or a single depository of documents or one particular event' [my emphasis]. In some respects it is as much a defining of the scope and scale of the research population as it is an approach to the research. Essentially it is a concentration on the specific rather than the general – a choice of depth over breadth. As such, it does not dictate a particular paradigm, nor does it preclude the use of any methodology, indeed it actively encourages a multi-method approach in order to gather the necessary depth and range of data, however, interviews or questionnaires, perhaps in the form of commissioned diaries, will often form a foundation.

Whilst a *survey* is often used as the collective term for the gathering of evidence via interviews and questionnaires (more of which in the next chapter), it is a distinct approach which seeks out relationships between variables and influential factors and trends over time – to compare and contrast. It has the potential to identify and explore 'cause and effect' without the need (or where it is not possible) to construct an experimental approach.

An *historical* approach seeks to explore the past to find explanations for contemporary issues or find solutions to current problems. Inevitably, as it is dealing with the past, it frequently finds itself connected to documentary evidence (that is, pre-existing data), but this is just one of many forms of recording of events in the multi-media age and the use of video or audio recordings should also be considered in addition to collecting primary data from those who experienced the situation first hand.

Generally (as there are several divergent views expressed in the literature here) *ethnographic* approaches are an attempt to reveal, describe and (in some cases) explain a culture that the intended audience of the research is unlikely to be familiar with in these terms. As an approach it is highly susceptible to the interpretations placed upon the evidence by the researcher. These interpretations will usually be revealed by the way that the evidence is selected or presented. *Feminist* research often adopts an ethnographic approach filtered through a particular editorial and philosophical perspective, with the aim of giving voice to the research participants. The *cultural* approach, as defined by Walliman (2005), concentrates on the way that a context can be interpreted and analysed through an examination of the linguistic content or through the interaction of language and the social setting (discourse analysis).

Evaluation can be taken to be the purpose of research activity, but Walliman (2005) argues that it should be considered a distinct approach with two separate strands. With *systems analysis* a holistic approach is taken to the examination of complex situation (classroom or organisational dynamics, for example), which is progressively deconstructed into more manageable (explainable) chunks. *Responsive evaluation* focuses on an impact analysis of initiatives (for example, a new scheme of work) on particular stakeholder groups (for example, students, teachers). Perceived in this way, it falls within the realms of the positivist paradigm, although the evaluation of the implementation of new programmes and initiatives may well justify a qualitative case study approach.

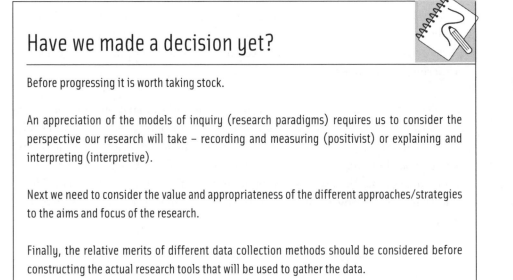

Have we made a decision yet?

Before progressing it is worth taking stock.

An appreciation of the models of inquiry (research paradigms) requires us to consider the perspective our research will take – recording and measuring (positivist) or explaining and interpreting (interpretive).

Next we need to consider the value and appropriateness of the different approaches/strategies to the aims and focus of the research.

Finally, the relative merits of different data collection methods should be considered before constructing the actual research tools that will be used to gather the data.

Let's see how this process might work in practice.

Deconstruct the question

As teachers we are repeatedly asked to start from the learning objectives and then work towards the construction of the learning activities and the delivery strategies (although there is increasing pressure to adopt particular teaching strategies and certain learning resources). In some key respects research activity has similar pressures. There may be an 'inner desire' to use a questionnaire or interview someone – but you have to hold yourself back from jumping in with a specific methodology and consider what is most appropriate for what you hope to achieve (your research aims).

We can start by examining some generic starting points for research activity and considering how they might be approached and what methods might be adopted. Look for similarities between the generic questions below and your own proposed piece of research.

How did we get to where we currently are?

Why are our exam results so poor? What makes our school so popular? What makes our staff (student) retention so bad?

◆ Either paradigm could be appropriate – positivism, if the aim is to detect a trend or pattern in relation to a particular phenomenon, or interpretivism, if the outcomes are to provide an insight into or a deeper understanding of it, including explanations.
◆ This type of focus strongly indicates a historical approach to examine factors and decisions to gain a deeper understanding of our current situation, but it might also be approached through a longitudinal study (if still contemporary) or as a case study.
◆ Methods are likely to include analysis of documents, questionnaires, interviews, focus group discussion.

Where are we?

How do we identify and address the needs of gifted and talented learners? How do we manage the performance of 'inadequate' teaching staff?

◆ Although an interpretive approach is possible, a mixed methodology including qualitative and quantitative data may generate a more complete picture.
◆ A static evaluation/examination of the current position in preparation for making a change would probably indicate a case study or survey approach. However, if the perceptions of the key players are the focus (the gifted learner/ the line manager/ the 'poor' teacher) then an ethnographic approach would be appropriate.

Continued

◆ Documents (policies and procedures) would offer reference points which could be compared with professional practice through interviews, observations or possibly participant diaries.

What are our options?

Which scheme is 'best' for our needs? Which mode of delivery will be most effective? What management structure should we choose?

◆ There is a positivist suggestion here of comparing opposing options in some criterion-referenced format, even so there will probably be a strong focus on the opinions of the stakeholders.
◆ As there is an emphasis on matching the appropriateness of differing potential lines of progression to current and proposed positions of a specific context, it is important to fully explore the nature of that context, suggesting a case study. However, the 'matching' element would probably suggest a survey approach to compare opinions.
◆ Evidence will be gathered from documents, to specify the options, and surveys and observation could be employed to gain greater understanding of the context.

What is happening?

What is induction like for a new member of staff? How do we manage the change towards vertical pastoral groups? What is actually involved in planning a residential trip?

◆ The passive tracking of a development through a focus on processes rather than outcomes does have a strong interpretive feel about it.
◆ Whilst an ethnographical approach may well provide a wider perspective of all the factors which impact on what is happening, a narrative approach may provide a much more personal perspective.

Continued

Once again documents (policies, etc) should provide a secure foundation on which to base discussion and analysis. Surveys should offer a wider perspective, whilst critical diaries can provide personal insights, with observation as a means of connecting the strands together.

What happens when we do this?

Does 'BrainGym' have an impact on learner concentration spans? What has been the effect on staff morale of 'learning teams'? What has been the impact of parental involvement in morning 'reading time'?

◆ Depending upon the specific interests of the researcher either paradigm is appropriate. In this case it is driven by the nature of the evidence being sought rather than the nature of the investigation itself.

◆ An interventionist approach to change, where the researcher manipulates the situations to progress towards a desired outcome as an iterative process, would suggest an action research approach. However, if it was approached from a more dispassionate and objective perspective, where the intervention, once started, was allowed to run its course, the approach would be more experimental in nature.

◆ Documents may provide an important 'base line' by which to judge the impact of subsequent initiatives – standardised test results, for example. However, it may be necessary to gather evidence through 'before and after' tests (surveys) or record change through participant observation. For more detailed and intimate responses and perceptions critical diaries should be considered alongside interview techniques.

What happened?

Did setting for maths improve the standardised test results? Has the personal tutorial system improved student retention? Did the peer mentoring system help to embed assessment for learning?

Continued

◆ Educational organisations frequently progress on to the 'next big initiative' before the effects of the previous one have been fully analysed and appreciated. Given this particular emphasis, the research module is likely to be positivist in attempting to accurately record the outcomes of an initiative.

◆ Evaluation of the effectiveness of a particular intervention or change strategy could be considered a *de post facto* approach. Adopting an evaluative approach suggests a more interventionist, or greater ownership of the issues than the first example given previously.

◆ Often documents will be useful in tracking what happened (minutes of meetings to lesson plans or examples of children's writing), but interviewing or distributing questionnaires to the key stakeholders would provide detailed and specific information about processes and the context within which they occur.

Working from pros and cons

The success of a research activity frequently hangs on the choice of an approach which appropriately meets the needs of the research aims. The examples offered provide an indication of the way that you need to be thinking to ensure that you think through the implications of what you are trying to achieve and that you are fully aware of the options available to you. If, for example, you are determined to compare the way that your school manages social inclusion with another school working with a similar intake, you need to consider very carefully issues of access to information – whilst your position in your school may mean that you have access to a full range of potential sources of information, you need to ask yourself whether you will be afforded similar access in the other school. Would, for example, a case study of your own school, linked to a review of policy documents publicly available from other schools be a more realistic and achievable approach?

Choosing a set of research methods is always a compromise between the ideal and the achievable, whilst maintaining a keen focus on the purposes of the research and its practicability. It is important to place any research on a secure foundation by ensuring that there will be the opportunity to access important sources of information – during the early stages of planning it is, therefore, essential that access is agreed to key sources, for example, documents held by the organisation, children in the focus class, parents/carers of the children, etc. Once the potential sources have been identified and access secured, it is then a matter of exploring the options for collecting appropriate evidence, of various types, from those sources.

The most frequently mentioned methods for gathering research evidence discussed and explained in the standard texts (Cohen *et al*, 2007; Bell, 2005; Denscombe, 2003, for example) include:

◆ observations;
◆ interviews;
◆ focus groups;
◆ questionnaires;
◆ documents;
◆ diaries; and
◆ tests.

Each one is examined in more detail in later chapters, along with a further examination of action research as a specific form of research in an educational setting. However, here is a brief listing of the key merits and drawbacks of each.

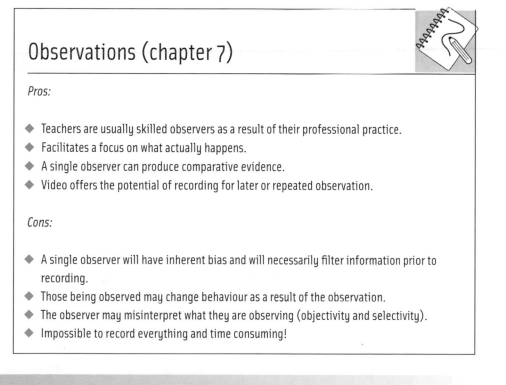

Observations (chapter 7)

Pros:

◆ Teachers are usually skilled observers as a result of their professional practice.
◆ Facilitates a focus on what actually happens.
◆ A single observer can produce comparative evidence.
◆ Video offers the potential of recording for later or repeated observation.

Cons:

◆ A single observer will have inherent bias and will necessarily filter information prior to recording.
◆ Those being observed may change behaviour as a result of the observation.
◆ The observer may misinterpret what they are observing (objectivity and selectivity).
◆ Impossible to record everything and time consuming!

Interviews (chapter 6)

Pros:

◆ Useful for obtaining sensitive or in-depth information from a knowledgeable respondent.
◆ Interactive – allows the interviewer to probe and pursue relevant themes.
◆ Most effective when there is a positive relationship and trust between interviewer and interviewee.

Cons:

◆ The interviewer requires the skill to keep the interview focused.
◆ Very time consuming, both to perform, record and collate.
◆ May be difficult to arrange.

Questionnaires (chapter 6)

Pros:

◆ Can generate a lot of information very quickly and easily.
◆ Can be structured to provide comparable information in an easily collatable form.
◆ Allows remote access to respondents.
◆ Provides respondent with privacy, anonymity and space for reflection.

Cons:

◆ Must be very carefully checked and trialled prior to use to ensure that instructions are unambiguous, responses are in the form expected and that it is manageable for the respondent.
◆ Response rate can be very low.
◆ Unlikely to obtain detailed or profound information this way.

Documents (chapter 8)

Pros:

◆ Useful as a base-line to other sources.
◆ Low cost and unobtrusive.
◆ Useful insight into past events.

Cons:

◆ Documents are unlikely to fit the precise needs of the research.
◆ Documents are not 'value neutral' and may have been written with a particular agenda or perspective in mind.
◆ Credibility and authenticity needs to be assured.

Diaries (chapter 6)

Pros:

◆ May provide detailed, insightful information over a period of time.
◆ May provide the basis for detailed interview.
◆ Comparative information from diarists (if a semi-structured approach is employed).

Cons:

◆ Significant effort, engagement and involvement required of the diarists.
◆ Non-standard responses/language/format can make comparisons.
◆ Diarists may be atypical or have their own agenda.

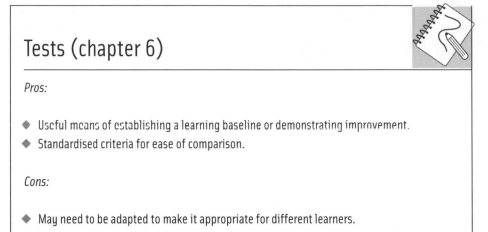

Tests (chapter 6)

Pros:

◆ Useful means of establishing a learning baseline or demonstrating improvement.
◆ Standardised criteria for ease of comparison.

Cons:

◆ May need to be adapted to make it appropriate for different learners.
◆ May not test the precise skills or knowledge under examination in the research.

Selection or de-selection?

Whilst it may be easier to explain why a certain research methodology has been chosen to gather specific information from a particular research population, it is perhaps more challenging to explain why others were rejected? For example, the choice of a semi-structured interview with the ICT coordinator/leader to discuss the implementation of a cross-curricular ICT initiative may be entirely reasonable and appropriate, but the decision would be much more secure if it could be shown that alternate methodologies were considered, but rejected for good reason. A critical diary, for the coordinator to complete during specific stages of the implementation process, whilst offering contemporaneous insights, may have been deemed too onerous or time consuming. But this at least demonstrates that the researcher is aware of other methods and can make rational decisions about how to proceed.

By approaching the final stages of the research design in this way it not only demonstrates your awareness of the options that you have available to you, and your knowledge of their strengths and weaknesses, but it also enables you to discuss this in close connection to the context of the research activity. This allows you to avoid having to resort to a 'textbook' style of explanation to demonstrate to your marking tutor just how much you know about research methodology in general but in relation to a specific practice setting.

To be able to understand the different research approaches sufficiently to be able to make informed and appropriate choices tends to suggest that you have taken the time and effort to read about them! It is important to acknowledge how your reading has influenced your decision-making process by making reference to these sources as you explain how you intend to gather your evidence.

Summary

Whilst it is not always necessary to progress through all of these stages, you should be aware of them so that you can appreciate their impact on the final construction and outcomes of your research activity. In your considerations you will demonstrate the influence of existing theories, different theoretical perspectives and conceptual constructions and past research in the field, along with an awareness and sensitivity to the context in which you are working and research population that you are working with.

Paradigm – what is your model or framework of inquiry?

Approach – what type of research strategy best fits what you hope to achieve?

Method – what are the most appropriate techniques for you to gather evidence?

From this, you then need to be able to construct *research tools* (observation/interview schedules, questionnaires) through which the evidence will actually be gathered.

FURTHER READING

◆ Bell, J., *Doing your Research Project*, Buckingham: Open University Press (2005)

◆ Briggs, A. J. R. and Coleman, M. (Eds) *Research Methods in Educational Leadership and Management* (2nd Ed) London: Sage Publications (2007)

◆ Cohen, L., Manion, L. and Morrison, K., *Research Methods in Education* (6th Ed) Abingdon: Routledge (2007)

◆ Denscombe, M., *The Good Research Guide* (2nd Ed) Maidenhead: Open University Press (2003)

◆ Taber K., *Classroom-based Research and Evidence-based Practice*, London: Sage Publications (2007)

6 How to Ask – Surveying the Situation

By the end of this chapter you should be able to:

◆ to recognise the strengths and weaknesses of questionnaires and interviews; and
◆ to determine the appropriateness of the approach for your research aims.

Based upon my own experience and of colleagues who have also supervised education research activity over a number of years, there is, undeniably, a 'magnetic' attraction between the novice researcher and the survey. It is as if there is some underlying perception that it 'isn't proper research' until a questionnaire has been distributed or interviewee sat down for interrogation. Whilst the survey is a useful technique for gathering comparative information from your research population, there are strengths and weaknesses that do need to be acknowledged and worked to.

Many texts on research methodology, as indicated in the previous chapter, list surveys as an approach to research, rather than a methodology for collecting evidence. Denscombe (2003) makes the explicit point that questionnaires and interviews are methodologies (among others) that are often associated with the survey approach. Whilst the survey focuses on comparing and contrasting the relationships between factors in a generalised way, the case study makes use of interviews and questionnaires to explore in depth and detail specifics. Clearly there is an issue here connected to the size of the research population that you are working with – small numbers will more naturally focus on specifics (case study), whilst larger numbers may allow generalised statements to be made with some degree of confidence (survey). Indeed, one of the most frequently asked questions of any supervisor of educational research must be: 'how many questionnaires/interviews should I do?', and the answer must always come back to the purpose of the study and overall size of the population that the research is focusing upon. Along with the balance of what is necessary to produce reliable results (see chapter 4) against what is practical and feasible for the researcher, the purpose of the research must always remain central to the discussions.

In this chapter questionnaires and interviews will be shown to be on a continuum with many more similarities than differences, even in terms of their presentation to the potential respondent.

What is a survey?

Bell (2005), after expressing some concern about the existence of a simple definition of a survey offers that it is where: 'all respondents will be asked the same questions in, as far as possible, the same circumstances' (p 14).

And goes on to suggest that success is more likely when those questions are of the: 'What? Where? When? and How?' (p 14) format. The same definition could almost have been used for a questionnaire, which does make the distinctions between the approach and the inherent methodologies difficult to clarify at this level. Denscombe (2003) attempts to overcome this by suggesting that the main characteristics of a survey is that it gathers evidence from a wide research population (where sampling may be required); can only represent a 'snap-shot' in time; and that it is empirical, in the sense that information will actually be collected and recorded. According to Cohen *et al* (2007) the main benefits of a survey are that it can be: 'used to scan a wide field of issues, populations, programmes, etc. in order to measure or describe any generalised features' (p 206).

Essentially, a survey should be defined in terms of the purpose to which the collected information will be put. There should be sufficient breadth of information to allow a comparative analysis, often statistical in nature, which will identify relationships and connections between different variables so that sub-groups within a population begin to stand out (statistically speaking). Morrison (1993) summarises these points effectively in stating that the survey approach:

◆ will gather evidence from a wide population, often necessitating the use of sampling;
◆ collects standardised information which can be collated, aggregated and statistically tested for relationships and correlations to check preconceived hypotheses against; and
◆ allows generalisations concerning relationships and patterns to be drawn.

Given that this is the purpose of a survey, it must be acknowledged that documentary analysis (chapter 8) would also be highly appropriate as a methodology to support this approach. However, it is apparent that there will be a close affinity between the survey as an approach and the questionnaire as the method.

What is a case study?

Case studies, as described in the previous chapter, by focusing on the specific, need to concentrate on generating a deep and detailed knowledge of a well-defined context or phenomenon. Frequently the case study researcher will rely upon the depth and valuable insights that can be revealed through a small number of highly focused interviews as a key methodological approach.

Links can often be found between case studies and surveys. The findings of a case study may be used as the justification for and foundation of a much wider survey to ascertain whether the specific findings have more general applicability. Conversely, the findings of a general survey may be explored in much greater depth and detail using a case study to put, as Bell (2005:10) describes it: 'flesh on the bones'.

Questionnaires and interviews

Both methods are based around asking questions of respondents, but the differences in presentation and format can become quite difficult to distinguish at the margins. Questionnaires are more suitable for larger populations, which are being asked to respond in short and simplified ways. Whereas interviews, due to logistical constrains, are really only appropriate for small populations but do, given the interactive nature, allow for a richer and more probing question format. The distinction can, at times, become quite artificial – if a researcher reads a questionnaire to a respondent and notes down the responses, does this automatically make it an interview? The same questions that can be read *by* an 11-year-old, will most likely need to be read *to* a 5-year-old.

Interviews and questionnaires will tend to have the same basic structure:

◆ *Biographical* – information about the respondent identifying factors which may be influential on subsequent responses (for example, gender, role, age, experience, qualifications, etc). Whilst names, or any other means of enabling a reader to identify individual respondents, will certainly not be included, for ethical reasons, in any presentation of the information, an individual identifier may be included here to allow you to go back to the respondent and check information at a later date.

◆ *Factual/opinions/perceptions* – information that you wish to gain from the respondent, using focused questions and statements derived from your conceptual reading around the initial research question.

◆ *Additional information* – any further information that the respondent can provide for you which is relevant to your student but has not been specifically requested elsewhere. Sometimes it is possible that the questions in the previous section have not allowed the respondent to tell you all that they know – this provides that opportunity.

As the researcher you have a couple of key variables to consider when constructing a research process which involves directly targeting a research population with questions to which you seek a response:

◆ the delivery format; and
◆ the question type.

To make the right choices for your particular context and research focus you need to be aware of the consequences of the decisions you are making.

The delivery format – questionnaires

An overview of the strengths and weaknesses were given in chapter 5 of specific forms of interview and questionnaire (including diaries and tests). Here we look at what options you have for getting your questions to, and your answers from, the potential research population. Purpose and population size are the first points to consider. If you are gathering information for comparative purposes and to examine possible relationships between factors then questionnaires or written tests (with or without sampling) would be the most appropriate starting point. If the information you are seeking is of a more detailed nature, particularly if it is specific to particular individuals or small groups, then some form of interview (group or individual), practical test or diary (in the case of collecting information over time) would be called for, again with sampling where necessary.

In the case of a questionnaire or 'written' test, once you have decided who will be receiving it (chapter 4 discusses research populations and sampling in more detail), then you need to consider which delivery/receipt system will be most effective for your particular context. The main ones available are:

By hand – if you have direct access to your research population (for example, learners in your classes, staff in your work team, parents attending teacher consultations) you can distribute the questionnaire personally to them, explaining the purpose of the research as you do so.

This personal touch, along with the provision of the facilities to complete the response (for example, pen, table, time!) can make a significant difference to the response rate. At the same time this does, potentially, throw up some ethical difficulties in terms of the researcher's relationship to the population; requiring a class to complete an evaluation form before they leave at the end of a session may well be 'normal' for the department or institution, but when those responses form part of a research methodology it is much less appropriate. It is also possible, in face-to-face (F2F) situations, to have group completion of questionnaires – for example different groups within a class completing a strengths, weaknesses, opportunities, threats (SWOT) analysis of a proposed change to the course they are on.

By (internal or external) mail – ideally all questionnaires should be distributed with a personalised covering letter and also include details of how and when the responses should be returned.

Most educational establishments have trays for internal mail and this could be utilised if you are researching within your own organisation. You will need to specify a date by which responses need to be returned to your tray. It is only worthwhile sending questionnaires to known individuals in other organisations; Verma and Mallick (1999) suggest that where post titles or impersonal 'Dear Madam/Sir' are used, the response rate is particularly low. You should always include a stamped, self-addressed envelope, for the anticipated response.

By electronic formats – there are two which are most frequently used; email attachment and web link. Both formats need to include a response to confirm that the attached explanation of the research and any instruction have been read and agreed.

A personalised email containing a questionnaire is often more appropriate than one sent through the post (and much cheaper!). In its simplest form it can be a

MsWord document that the respondent downloads, completes and returns as an attachment. However, having the questionnaire on a linked web page is much easier for the respondent and can also be constructed so that the information is automatically downloaded to a spreadsheet ready for analysis. Alternatively, using virtual learning environments, such as Blackboard or FirstClass groups or cohorts can be sent invitations to complete online questionnaires or tests which are automatically collated for the researcher. To construct an 'online' questionnaire not only do you need to carefully consider the content and structure, but you also need to ensure that it appears on screen correctly. This web-based approach does require considerable effort to set up and get to the research population in the first place and is only really appropriate if they are already making use of it for other purposes.

The delivery format – interviews

Depending on the levels of technology available to you and your research population, there are four main formats available to you for interviewing: F2F, telephone, video conferencing and online. A further complication being that as well as individual interviews, you could also consider the possibility and benefits of group interviews. Finally, the delivery format will also impact on the options you have for recording the outcomes of the interview.

In interviews, much of the biographical data can be collected without the need to ask direct questions (gender), but others are worth asking brief questions and be sure that the interviewee is made aware that these are brief, otherwise a: 'how long have you been doing this job?' could give you a complete, but unwanted, career history.

Interviews are only really worthwhile when they are interactive (or the literacy of the individual is such that they would be unable to complete a questionnaire) so the format and the structure of the interview should work to those strengths. As interviews can be quite time consuming for both the interviewer and the interviewee it is imperative that both sides are fully briefed as to the purpose and the value of the potential evidence from the interviewee.

F2F – the 'traditional' format for interviews where the interviewer and interviewee pre-arrange a date, time, place and focus for the face-to-face interview. It generally is most effective when the interviewer goes to the interviewee, particularly if it is 'neutral ground', convenient for the interviewee, but away from distractions.

This approach is particularly appropriate for accessing key information from an important individual who, perhaps, has a unique perspective of the issues under consideration. Care must be taken in your choice of recording techniques, and should always be agreed in advance with the interviewee. Videoing the interview can be very intimidating leading to a loss of spontaneity and detail, but it does mean that as much of the event as possible has been captured for future analysis (including non-verbal communication). However, this will leave the interviewer with a mass of information to transcribe and analyse. Audio recording will be less intrusive but will not collect non-verbal communications and will still have the same transcription and analysis problems, which will be exacerbated if the recording is indistinct or different respondents are talking in a group situation. Contemporaneous note-taking will inevitably split the concentration of the interviewer (between the notes and the interviewee) and, at best, will only be a partial record. The written record will be based upon what appeared to be important to the interviewer at the time and selectivity may subsequently be revealed to be flawed. Apart from the need to 'write the notes up' directly after the interview, this approach is very time-efficient for the researcher and can gather the key information very effectively, including both direct quotes and general evidence.

Video conferencing – whilst it may save on travel time and costs it can be an expensive option and does require that both 'ends' of the interview have the necessary technology and skills available to them. It does mean that more geographically distant potential respondents can be approached.

With the increasing availability and use of webcam technology, this approach may become increasingly popular, particularly with the requisite Internet speeds available at most educational establishments. It continues to allow non-verbal communication but the use of the technology may be daunting for some, resulting in a less 'relaxed' interview. Video recording of the interview will be no more intrusive than the process itself, but the issues concerning transcription remain.

Telephone interview – chosen for many of the same reasons as the video conference, but much more 'low-tech' and consequently less threatening and easier to arrange.

Whilst the 'manner' of the interviewer is important in all forms of interview, in terms of putting the interviewee at ease, encouraging them to discuss the issues in question with openness and confidence, all the interviewer has in a telephone interview is the tone of their voice and the language used. It is not so easy to smile and nod gently through a telephone to encourage an interviewee to continue, or to 'wrinkle your brow' in order to get your interviewee to explain the last point in more depth! Effective interviewing is a skill that needs to be developed and practiced. Asking the right questions are only part of the formula, how you ask them is just as important – as the researcher this is something that you will need to practice before you try it for real.

Online – use of a web-based 'chat room' as the location for your interview.

Whilst there are many strengths to this approach, including access to more distant respondents and the potential of having a lasting record of the interview, it does require a very different set of interviewing skills and the need to ascertain precisely who the respondent is when you are working via an open portal (that is, one not based around, for example, membership of a course via a virtual learning environment (VLE). As with the other technology-based interview approaches mentioned above, both the interviewer and the interviewee need to be confident and comfortable with the format.

The diary

One final form of 'interview' (or questionnaire, depending how it is perceived and presented) is the commissioned diary. For this to work effectively and have value in a piece of focused research, the diarist needs to be appropriately briefed for both purpose and format. The formats of diaries can vary enormously from time delayed questionnaires focusing explicitly on information (an educator being asked to record at the end of each day the approximate amount of time they have spent of different educational activities – teaching (groups), teaching (individuals), planning, marking) to a much more 'open' format ('what were your highlights and lowlights in class today?) – more on constructing questions. Depending upon the nature and focus of the study, the duration may also vary significantly from a snapshot, but detailed, day, to a weekly learning diary (a PGCE student, for example) lasting the duration of their course (a ten-month period in this case).

The diary may be presented in the traditional 'written' format or make use of same form of electronic transmission. The easiest to set-up would be to email the diary questions to the respondents on a regular basis for them to respond to, however a blog (web log), once set up, allows the respondent to communicate more freely.

Constructing an interview schedule

'One major advantage of the interview is its adaptability', Bell (2005:157) claims with good reason. The key benefit of the interview over the questionnaire is dependent upon the interviewer's ability to respond to the answers that the interviewee gives and to take the interview in different directions as a result. The openness of the questions within the schedule lies at the heart of this so that an interview will lie somewhere on a continuum from *structured* to *unstructured*.

Structured interviews – the interviewer works methodically through an interview schedule which is usually composed of closed or multiple-choice questions. The advantage over a paper-based questionnaire is an increased response rate, and that it gives the interviewer the opportunity of working through a large schedule on a 'critical path' basis (that is, if the answer to question 4 is 'a', go to section 7 – which might be very difficult to follow as a questionnaire). Essentially you are recording the interviewee's responses to a questionnaire.

Semi-structured interviews – a more flexible style can be used to collect equivalent information. You will need to begin by identifying a number of key questions focusing on the theme of your study to act as prompts. Dependent upon the response that you receive you will then either ask further questions to pursue fruitful lines of enquiry in more detail or move on to the next key question.

Unstructured interviews – they may be used in exploring an area in preliminary research (as you are still attempting to locate or establish an explicit focus for your study), or at a later stage for particular people with access to specialised information or will be able to provide you with a crucial and unique perspective on an issue (such as the departmental, course or subject leader). A few key questions may be prepared in advance, but it is mainly about setting up the opportunity for the respondent to tell you what they know about the issues relevant to your study. To do this successfully, you, as the interviewer, will need to:

1. Possess, and possibly demonstrate, considerable background knowledge (show that you know what you are talking about and that you understand any specialised terminology being used – this is where the background reading is so essential once more!).
2. Use informed questioning (based on the ideas and research findings from your reading).
3. React with sensitivity to new leads (don't get over enthusiastic at responses!).

Once you have determined the structure (or combination) that would best suit your purposes with your particular respondents you then need to consider, specifically, the format of the questions you intend to ask, and how you would like your interviewee to respond. Tuckman (1972) offers seven different response modes, of which 'structured' and 'unstructured' are most relevant to interviewing (the other five are more appropriate to questionnaire formats). Using a structured approach limits the response from the interviewee, for example:

'why did you ask the class to work in friendship groups?' – unstructured; and

'can you give two reasons to explain why you asked the class to work in friendship groups?' – structured (limited to two reasons).

Bell (2005) provides an example of a structured response linked to follow-up questions concerning participation in a specific programme where the responses are limited to:

1. not at all (any particular reasons?);
2. to a certain extent (ask for examples); and
3. a great deal (ask for examples) (p 160).

It is also useful to consider the questions from a process perspective as suggested by Kvale (1996), identifying questions that:

◆ introduce the theme of the study to the interviewer;
◆ ask for information;
◆ ask for an example;
◆ probe and follow up a response; and
◆ interpret and reformulate a response (clarify and check understanding) (p 133–5).

Denscombe (2003:179) take the process one stage further by linking the prompts, probes and checks to interviewer behaviours: the interviewer can encourage the interviewee to respond by remaining silent, repeating the question or the last few words of the response, or asking for examples.

Clearly there is a link between the format of the interview and how structured it needs to be centred on the depth of information that is expected or being sought.

Interview schedule – the research tool

Case Study 6.1 Tutor engagement with building learning power (BLP) techniques in their teaching

---

'Learning Advocate' responsible for staff training for BLP (MA student) 'Rasool'

Interview schedule:

Section 1
Note down personal details – role, age, experience, qualifications, training, etc.

Section 2
Have you made much use of BLP techniques in your teaching?
None/minimal – go to list A
Some/moderate – go to list B
Lots – go to list C
A – What has prevented you? What help do you need? What could you do?
B – Examples? What more could you do? What is hindering you?
What is helping?
C – Examples? Why has it been so successful? How would you encourage others?

Section 3
What other comments do you have about BLP? Support and training?

Case Study 6.1 is an example of a semi-structured (bordering on structured) approach using differentiated questions.

Case Study 6.2   Evaluating the effect of giving written feedback to KS2 learners in a large primary school

New deputy headteacher (MA student) 'Nina'

Interviews with a representative sample of KS2 children, their tray of books is available as a stimulus

Section 1
Note down personal details – gender, age, general ability, etc

Section 2
How do you know how well you are doing?
How do you know what you need to do next?

Section 3
Would you want to change the way we give you feedback in any way?

Case Study 6.2 adopts a much more open strategy and uses a stimulus (the books) which, in this case, can also be used to identify examples.

Constructing a questionnaire

A well constructed questionnaire is one where the researcher has done the work so as to reduce the effort on the part of the respondent. A highly structured questionnaire which limits the possible responses speeds up the completion, collation and analysis and makes the whole process much more manageable for all concerned. A questionnaire consisting of a 'tell me all you know about …' request and a blank page would be very daunting to complete and very time consuming to code and collate. Open-ended questions are much better placed as a final 'catch all' – 'is there anything else you can tell me about …. which wasn't covered elsewhere?' can be quite helpful.

Cohen *et al* (2007:322) identify seven types of question, which can also be linked to the type of data that will be produced and most appropriate data presentation formats.

Table 6.1 ◆ Types of question

Question type	Example	Data form	Graphical presentation
Dichotomous	Gender, yes/no	Categoric	Pie chart
Multiple-choice (single response)	School type, banded responses	Categoric	Pie chart
Multiple-choice (multiple response)	Resources used, topics taught	Categoric	Bar chart
Rating scales	Likert scale responses	Ordinal	Pie chart, bar chart
Rank order	Importance or preference	Ordinal	Bar chart
Constant sum	Distribute 'ten' points between a set of options	Ordinal	Bar chart
Ratio data	Age in years	Continuous	Line graph
Open ended	Comment on; Explain	Text	None – except where coded, collated and categorised

Dichotomous – where there are only two options. Very limited; as they do not allow for 'grey areas' so should only be used for questions such as male/female, rather than: 'are you a good teacher? – yes/no'!

Multiple-choice (single) – where only one response is possible; for example,

> How many years have you worked here? 0–5 ☐ 6–10 ☐ 11–15 ☐ 16+ ☐

Can be used to give a simplified categoric response (tick a box rather than write something).

Multiple-choice (multiple) – where more than one response is possible; for example,

> Which curriculum subjects have you taught this year: maths ☐ science ☐ English ☐ geog ☐ hist ☐ DT ☐ PE ☐ art ☐ music ☐ ICT ☐ Other.................. ☐ (tick all applicable).

With multiple-choice responses it is sometimes necessary to include an 'other (please state) ……' category in case you have missed an option!

Rating scales – enables the respondent to indicate a level of 'feeling', 'intensity' or 'confidence' (preferable to yes/no). The Likert scale, originally devised by Renis Likert, needs to be well-defined with the same key word being used for each point of the scale – 'never, seldom, sometimes, occasionally, often, always' lacks precision and differentiation. Using statements rather than questions and a scale based upon the level of agreement can offer a consistent and meaningful approach; for example,

---

The literacy levels of our new students has increased in recent years

SD ☐   D ☐   A/D? ☐   A ☐   SA ☐ (using Strongly Disagree to Strongly Agree)

Generally ratings scales focus upon opinions and perceptions about issues rather than supplying factual information. Rather than using the Likert approach you might want to consider using a simple 10-point scale (poor to excellent) which can be used to rate factors such as:

| The quality of learning resources | 1 2 3 4 5 6 7 8 9 10 |
| Appropriateness of teaching techniques | 1 2 3 4 5 6 7 8 9 10 |

Rank order – useful for identifying orders of importance or priority from the range of options provided; for example, departmental objectives for the year or factors which need to be taken into account when planning a practical activity. It is possible to compare the relative ranking by different groups (males/females; teachers/managers) using Spearman's rank correlation coefficient.

Place the following factors in order of importance to you for your job from 1 (most important) to 10 (least)

Good wages   ☐

Job security   ☐

Continued

Personal loyalty to employees	☐
Work that keeps you interested	☐
Feeling 'in' on things	☐
Good working conditions	☐
Appreciation of work done	☐
Promotion and growth within the school	☐
Sympathetic help on personal problems	☐
Tactful disciplining	☐

Constant sum – this can show the scale of difference between options rather than just the order. Rather simply placing the most 'important' option as ranked first, it can be given, for example, seven out of ten points leaving just three to be distributed between the other four options (that is, it is *much* more important than the others!).

Demonstrate the importance of the following factors to you for your job by distributing ten 'votes' between them – for example, if they are all of equal value, give them one vote each, if only one factor is of any importance, give it ten.	
Good wages	☐
Job security	☐
Personal loyalty to employees	☐
Work that keeps you interested	☐
Feeling 'in' on things	☐
Good working conditions	☐
Appreciation of work done	☐
Promotion and growth within the school	☐

Continued

Sympathetic help on personal problems	☐
Tactful disciplining	☐ votes must total ten

Ratio data – this represents pure numerical data, such as test scores, class size, teaching hours and 'settling down time'. This allows full use of statistical tests for averages and dispersion.

Open-ended questions – These questions are phrased in such a way as to allow the respondent to answer in their own words. Their responses may be limited in length by providing a box for the respondent to write in:

What, for you, were the benefits of the mentoring process?

Common themes within the responses might be able to be identified to allow for a degree of collation. The key strength of this form of response though is that it allows you to select quotations to emphasise points that you wish to make within your analysis and provide 'colour' for your presentation of your findings.

Questionnaire – the research tool

When you develop a questionnaire you should ensure that the questions:

◆ are unambiguous;
◆ have a clear and simple focus (avoid double questions);
◆ are short;
◆ use common language;
◆ avoid the use of double negatives; and
◆ do not lead the respondents into particular answers.

Always trial your questionnaires to ensure that they meet these criteria and provide you with the information that you need. Whilst you should endeavour to use a range of question types, you should not jump from one type to another without providing adequate instructions. Try to have blocks of similar ones, but vary statements between positive and negative to avoid the respondent ticking the same box each time (make them think!).

FURTHER READING

◆ Bell, J., *Doing Your Research Project* (4th Ed) Buckingham: Open University Press (2005)

◆ Denscombe, M., *The Good Research Guide* (2nd Ed) Maidenhead: Open University Press (2003)

◆ Fogelman, K. and Comber, C., 'Surveys and Sampling in Briggs', A. J. R. and Coleman, M. (Eds) *Research Methods in Educational Leadership and Management* (2nd Ed) London: Sage Publications (2007)

◆ Walliman, N., *Your Research Project*, London: Sage Publications (2005)

How to Ask – Observing Operations and Outcomes

By the completion of this chapter you should be able to:

◆ recognise the strengths and weaknesses of observation and the recording of observations to determine the appropriateness of the approach; and
◆ construct observation schedules suitable to the context and the conceptual focus of the research.

Observation can be one of the most powerful tools in research and this is especially true for practitioner researchers in the social sciences. The training and experience of those engaged in the caring professions requires close attention to the details of their professional context. For instance, teachers must constantly monitor the progress of children in relation not only to their academic development but also the progress of social skills and general behaviour. Teachers quite naturally observe children on a minute by minute basis, or over the longer term, in order to make sure that their methods of teaching are effective and that children are on task and engaged in their learning. For other professions such as nursing and social work, the observation of patient or client is central to professional processes which are part of the job. The creation of national regimes of accountability, such as that practised by Ofsted, are based on a methodology that has at its heart the process of systematic observation to judge the quality of individual teachers and schools. Increasingly within-school activities have also employed forms of observation as part of mentoring and coaching activities or for performance review. It, therefore, follows that educational professionals should have the prerequisite skills, so to ensure that, as a methodology, it is employed to good effect.

The 'natural' research tool of the educational profession?

For the many reasons why observation comes naturally to many, if not all, of those undertaking research in educational settings, it is really surprising how infrequently observation forms part of the research methodology. There are three main reasons for this. First, the reluctance to integrate observation into an approach is a hang-over from notions that research should be 'scientific' in character and many researchers seem to feel that simply looking at what is going on around them will not be viewed as 'good research'. This is, of course, somewhat ironic, since observation has been central to the scientific method, especially in the biological sciences, for hundreds of years. Second, 'familiarity breeds contempt' and many aspirant researchers are reluctant to use research tools which they employ every day in their professional lives, sometimes quite understandably, because they wish to try out other less familiar and more esoteric research techniques. Third, and finally, there is often a concern that observational approaches will be time-consuming and that research tools will be complex and difficult to develop. Again, this last point is quite understandable since the kind of unstructured everyday observation that practitioners undertake as part of their work may not seem appropriate for a formal research project which may have both money and personal prestige invested into it.

Observation can, nonetheless, be used as part of any number of research approaches and is one of the most flexible means of conducting research:

◆ Comparatively unstructured observation can be employed as part of a highly qualitative approach to research. It can be employed to support diary writing as part of one or more of the interpretive paradigms.
◆ Systematic observation can lead on to the use of statistical analysis as a means of calculating frequencies that may lead to generaliseable conclusions about events that may assist in the analysis of learning success or failure, behaviour modification, the comparative efficacy of 'treatment' or social adaptation and change.
◆ Observation can be employed as one element of a blended or mixed methods approach and can be employed as a first research tool that provides the basis for subsequent positivist research tools, or as a second research tool that will add richness to the data gathering process, or can be operated simultaneously with other research approaches and thus allowed to both inform and be informed by other data gathering techniques.

Types and forms of observation

Figure 7.1 lists the relative merits of observational methods.

Observation is especially helpful in providing deep, rich data that provide verisimil-
itude to the research process since: 'it provides a degree of life experience that
is lacking in most academic environments' (Hammersley, 1993: 197). Thody (2006:
133) suggests that observation is especially useful in the 'openings' to research reports
since it is unrivalled in attracting reader attention and in establishing the atmosphere
of the context within which the research took place. Whether used as an opening
that leads on to other types of data collection and analysis or as the totality of the
method employed, it is undoubtedly true that observation is unrivalled in enabling
the researcher to immerse themselves in the research environment and correlatively
in drawing the reader into the world of the researcher and researched. For these
reasons observation is fundamental to the processes of ethnographic methods and is
also often associated with the grounded theory approaches made famous by Glaser
and Strauss (1967). The increasing use of first person narrative in research reports
and theses has enabled observation to come to the fore in both undergraduate and
post-graduate research. Not too many years ago such methods of reporting and
writing-up would have been frowned upon by many in the academic community
but such responses are now, thankfully, rare. Anyone researching the complex social
setting of the classroom, the home or other caring contexts will need to consider
whether observation should form part of their approach.

Observation can enable the research to gather data on a range of settings including the physical setting (the physical environment of the organisation); the human

Advantages	Disadvantages	Paradigm	Uses
Can reveal behaviours and characteristics and group interactions that the subject/ respondent may not themselves be aware of.	Time consuming and lengthy and subjective in interpretation.	Largely qualitative but observation schedules can include carefully thought out mapping techniques that are susceptible to quantitative analysis.	Especially appropriate for examining teacher–pupil/ pupil–pupil interactions in the classroom, playground or other social situation.

Fig. 7.1 ◆ Applicability of observational methods

setting (the way people are organised, the numbers and types of people that are employed); the interactional setting (the forms of interactions and exchanges that are taking place and the ways they are planned); and, the programme setting (such as resources, teaching or other professional styles or approaches) (Morrison, 1993: 80). Even more importantly observation can take several forms (Cohen, Manion and Morrison, 2000: 305) which are listed below (Fig. 7.2):

In slight contrast Robson (1993: 316–319) distinguishes between the *complete participant*, where the observer actually conceals that they are a researcher in order to become a full member of a group; the *participant as observer*, where the researcher makes clear that they are observing the situation from the start but still tries to establish close relationships with the group; the *marginal participant*, where the researcher adopts a largely passive role merely watching what is going on, but is

Form of observation	Key features
Highly structured	The researcher works out exactly what features they are looking for prior to commencing observation. Observation categories will have been worked out and structured observational tools will have been developed to record data. Observation will be highly systematic and methods of analysis are likely to be statistical.
Semi-structured	The researcher will have worked out the main issues that they wish to explore and so will have a clear conception of what it is they wish to observe. The observational tool used to record data will also be worked out in advance but is likely to allow note-taking rather than highly structured responses. Observation will be semi-systematic and methods of analysis are likely to be qualitative, although some basic numeric analysis may be undertaken.
Unstructured	The researcher will only have a generalised conception of what is to be observed, probably relating to an overall research theme or issue. Research tools for recording data are likely to be unstructured are likely to take the form of notes. Methods of analysis will be qualitative.

Fig. 7.2 ◆ Forms of observation

nonetheless a participant in the group; and, the *observer-as-nonparticipant* where the researcher takes no part in the activity whatsoever, although their role is known throughout. Such a continuum will reflect the nature of the research being carried out and will almost certainly imply whether the researcher wishes to operate within the interpretive or positivist paradigms with consonant effects on methods of analysis. For instance, the complete participant is most likely to be engaged in some form of highly ethnographic process whereby the researcher wishes to be immersed fully within a particular culture. At the other extreme, the observer-as-nonparticipant, is far more likely to be interested in scientific or a semi-scientific approach that will enable appropriate statistical procedures to be applied to the data that is gathered.

In choosing which type of observation to undertake, the researcher will draw on a range of variables in order to make their decision which will include their research aims and which method is most likely to fulfil them; their background training and whether it predisposes them to qualitative or quantitative approaches; the access that they are likely to be able gain to the group; and even their ethical standpoint with regard to informing those under observation of their intentions.

Ask yourself

What methods of observation do you employ during your professional practice? How do you analyse such observations? Are any of the processes you use 'formal' and 'systematic'?

What problems might you encounter if tried to employ observation in your current (or a related) work setting? What sensitivities would you encounter? Who might object?

Research tools and methods of recording data

The flexibility of the observational method means that an extremely wide variety of data recording approaches may be employed. The nature of such tools will depend in the original aims of the research project and the intended research paradigm or paradigms that the researcher intends to operate within. Crucially, the research tool must be structured in such a way as to enable the methods of analysis that the researcher intends to employ. For this reason methods of recording will vary widely within the method according to the skills, training and personal predilections of the researcher. Indeed observation is an area of research which enables the widest set of approaches of almost any of the many approaches available to the researcher. Even a general research text such as Cohen, Manion and Morrison (2000: 311–313) lists two detailed pages of methods of recording, whilst, similarly, Sarantakos (1998: 214–217) offers almost three pages on the topic. These include approaches such as:

◆ quick jottings of key words or the use of symbols;
◆ detailed note-taking or field notes which may be on pre-determined themes or in response to events as they unfold;
◆ pen portraits of participants;
◆ descriptions of events, behaviour or activities;
◆ 'chronologs' describing events or episodes along with the time of occurrence or recording of observations at predetermined times;
◆ context maps, sketches or other non-verbal representations;
◆ rating scales, checklists or taxonomies; and
◆ sociometric diagrams that indicate relationships between people or show key shifts in control such as the changing speakers in a staff meeting.

At their simplest the recording of observation may take place through simple jottings in a diary which may note phenomena as they occur. Some researchers employ new diaries for this purpose, others merely use footnotes in general diaries – although one would expect that such an *ad hoc* approach would form just one element in a more carefully constructed approach. The paramount concern is that important events or occurrences are captured and that the chronology is captured so that the evolution of patterns can be determined. Contemporaneous diary writing will provide an opportunity to record observations in an extremely rich form that will be especially useful in the more reflexive forms of research. The advent of accountability activities such as appraisal and performance management has increased the prevalence of observation activities as a normal part of institutional life. For this reason researchers frequently adopt an observation schedule that enables structured observation according to key themes in a manner which is reminiscent of the Ofsted approach. Figure 7.3 offers an example of such an observational tool that focuses on curriculum development and might be employed by a researcher interested in the efficacy of certain curricula approaches, innovations or action

Curriculum development observation research project		
Name of observer:	**Individual observed:**	
Group observed:		
Date:	**Time:**	
Focus of lesson:		
Quality of teaching and learning and of the curriculum:		
Pupils' attitudes, values and personal development:		
Classroom management:		
General observations:		

Fig. 7.3 ◆ Curriculum development observation schedule

research activities. A simple form such as this should contain key information such as the names of the observer and observed, the date and time and provide a matrix for note-taking against pre-determined themes that relate to research aims.

A modified version of such a schedule is suitable for critical incident/critical event observation. Such events or occurrences are deemed to be particularly important

Critical event analysis	
Critical event number:	**Name of teacher:**
Group/ class:	
Date:	**Time:**
Focus of event:	

What precipitated the event:

What took place:

Outcomes:

Notes on interviews with participants:

Fig. 7.4 ◆ Critical event analysis schedule

since they may typify or illuminate a particular feature of organisational culture or social interaction. Such approaches are most often employed by those interested in behaviour management, student integration problems, or issues relating to the student-student, client-client or staff-client interface, Fig. 7.4.

Some academic commentators, such as Bryman (2004) emphasise a more systematic approach to observation with a concomitant requirement for an observation schedule with clear focus, and simple system of recording that takes account of subsequent systems of coding of data and show due consideration for reliability and validity (Bryman, 2004: 169–170). Such approaches will enable highly structured methods that may employ diacritical marks to record events in a manner which will be familiar to those trained in psychology. For instance, Fig. 7.5 provides an apparently simple representation of how much time off-task individuals in a group of ten children spent during a ten-minute period of observation. The chart will provide a very straightforward numeric representation of the number of occasions when children failed to pay attention to their work. At first sight the chart may seem to be useful in providing a fairly precise indication of which children within the group are attentive to their work and which are not. However, such a schematic representation might lead to a series of other important questions. For instance, children numbers 1 and 5 seem to be off-task for the greatest amount of time during the 15 minutes of observation but does the chart give a hint as to why they were off task? For instance, is child number 3 instigating an interaction that may cause a breakdown in concentration? Why is child number 7 apparently attentive until the final minutes of the period of observation? Has she, for instance completed all the work given to her and has become bored? Why does child number 9 appear to be on-task for most of the period but have brief periods when she is off-task and then, apparently, get back to work? Such questions are tantalising and cannot be answered by such a chart in isolation. They need to be followed up by further observation (Fig. 7.6) which may focus on types or forms of interaction of only one or two individuals at a time, in a way that will allow for much more detailed qualitative analysis. This is not to say that such an observation chart is not of value in itself. In its own right it will provide clear and precise indications of the length of time that a particular individual or a whole group of children are undertaking a particular task and this can be analysed through the use of simple statistical techniques in a way that may inform the researcher about the efficacy and interest levels of particular curricula approaches or pieces of work. The technique could be employed as a pre- and post- test to see whether some change in materials or pedagogic technique encouraged engagement by pupils. Or it could be used as one in a variety of methods to investigate complex sets of relationships amongst children.

Minor modifications to such a chart enable it to be used for very different purposes. So, instead of measuring 'negative' activities such as time-off task the observations could be to see the extent to which young children are socialising and cooperating in their work.

		Time in one minute intervals														
		1	2	3	4	5	6	7	8	9	1	1	1	1	1	1
Name of child	1.		X	X	X				X	X	X	X				
	2. Diane															
	3. Neil	X						X	X							
	4. Chris			X											X	X
	5.		X	X	X	X	X	X								
	6. Jane															
	7. Pat												X	X	X	X
	8.															
	9. Hattie						X					X				
	10. Paul									X	X	X				

X indicates time-off task

Fig. 7.5 ✦ Chart of time off-task over a 15-minute period

		Socialisation/interaction level			
		High	**Medium**	**Low**	**Notes**
Time in five minutes intervals	10.00				
	10.05				
	10.10				
	10.15				
	10.20				
	10.25				
	10.30				

Fig. 7.6 ✦ Socialisation/interaction level

Ask yourself

What would be the key features of an observation schedule for a small-scale project relevant to your own professional context? Is the schedule susceptible to quantitative or qualitative data analysis or both?

Methods of analysis of observational data

The forms of observation that are susceptible to qualitative analysis may be addressed either by the use of 'traditional' methods of data interrogation or through the use of the increasing number of electronic data analysis packages. The decision whether to employ electronic means is both individual and pragmatic. Some experienced researchers continue to use manual means even if they have the skills to employ electronic approaches since they wish to remain in close personal contact with the data whilst others regularly use electronic means even when exploring comparatively small amounts of material. However, a general rule is that small-scale pieces of research that have elicited comparatively little qualitative data may not be worth the time and effort of coming to grips with the complexities of an electronic approach unless learning such techniques is in itself a goal of the researcher. Whether using electronic or manual means the essence of qualitative analysis remains the same: to look for key commonalities within the data that indicate; linkages, illuminate research questions or point to emerging themes within the data. This process is facilitated by close reading of the material that has been derived from observation and where this is in the form of notes, diary or other verbal means of recording the researcher will seek to allocate key phrases, utterances or incidents to pre-determined or emergent themes or nodes. The process might follow a straightforward path of transcription of original notes and primary data followed by close reading of the material during which the main concepts are highlighted, either manually or electronically and the resulting material is categorised and ordered. A simple stem and branch analysis would include the creation of key themes from original research objectives which might then form the basis of a series of matrices with emergent sub-themes.

Wragg (1999) suggests caution to those untrained in statistical approaches and to consult a statistician rather than to misuse a procedure. However, he suggests that the following techniques are the most common and most appropriate ways of analysing observational data through statistical methods:

Relationships between measures – used to calculate the relationship between two measures such as the amount of misbehaviour and the number of pupils applying themselves to a task.

Comparing groups – dependant on the type of measure involved. If a frequency count has been taken a chi square may be appropriate but other techniques such as a t test, Mann-Whitney U or Kruskal-Wallis analysis may be appropriate.

Measuring change – especially useful in calculating 'value-added' and thus for comparing the progress of unmatched groups.

Predicting – multiple regression analysis.

Reducing complexity – factor analysis or cluster analysis.

Aggregating findings – used to put together findings from several different pieces of observational research. Most commonly associated with 'meta-analysis'.

(Wragg, 1999: 123–127)

A chapter on observation is not itself the place for a detailed outline of either qualitative or statistical techniques of analysis but there are a range of excellent texts that provide detailed instructions on where and how to apply such approaches that are accessible to the non-specialist. Those interested in qualitative approaches might examine the work of Miles and Huberman (1994) or Silverman (2004) whilst those seeking guidance on quantitative approaches could see, for instance, Solomon and Winch (1993); Clegg (1994); Cohen and Holiday (1996); or, Bryman and Cramer (1997).

Ethics and observational methods

It is easy to overlook ethical issues when employing observational techniques since observational methods do not employ intervention and may be perceived to be part of 'normal professional duties'. Nonetheless, as noted earlier, observation may be employed as a result of critical incidents or may be the precursor to intervention as part of an action research cycle. Even when disassociated from intervention the act of observation is itself a matter of extreme sensitivity since it will involve at least an element of judgement-making; which may be deemed to be sensitive within the social context of the workplace. For instance, when observing a classroom judgements may be made about the quality of teaching and learning, thus potentially impugning the professional competence of the colleague observed or the abilities of the student. Moreover, any observation of child subjects will always contain potential problems since child protection issues will be paramount. For this reason the permissions for ethical research should be sought, as explained in chapter 4, as a 'precaution'. Additionally it is crucial to recognise and acknowledge that observation as part of research processes should never be confused with observation for accountability or other managerial processes. This should form part of the 'contract' between the observer and the observed so there should be no doubt that data gathered in the process of research observation will be used solely for the purposes of the research project and will not be employed as part of competence or capability procedures.

Intervention?

The subject of whether or not to intervene during the process of observation is a vexed one and is not infrequently the subject of lively discussion and conjecture amongst academic colleagues involved in such data-gathering processes. Of course, there are not real issues if the researcher has chosen to undertake the role of 'participant observer' since intervention, discussion and engagement form part of the research process. The situation is far more complex for the non-participant observer who determines to operate as without taking part in the activity that is the focus of observation. The nub of the issue usually revolves around when and whether it is appropriate to interject if the observer sees something occur, or about to occur, that is inappropriate or dangerous. There are several disadvantages to such intervention including the fact that the researcher will inevitably cease to function as a researcher since they will themselves become part of the activity under scrutiny. Further, any such intervention may be very distressing to those being observed since it may be seen to imply some lack of ability by those in charge of the activity being observed. All researchers will face such a situation at some time during the process of observational research and they will make a professional decision whether or not to act to intercede based on circumstance. In general the decision will focus on whether there is likelihood of injury, whether physical or emotional, to the subjects.

Conclusions

Observation is one of the most powerful and most overlooked of research approaches. Frequently those undertaking research projects in the Social Sciences, have finely honed skills in observation through years of training and professional practice within which the scrutiny of colleagues and, most importantly, clients, pupils or students, forms an integral part of their role. The use of observation does not predetermine or even imply the dominant research tradition within which the researcher intends to work since data gathered through such methods can be employed as part of either a positivist or interpretive approach to data interrogation. Such decisions about paradigmatic approaches will, however, be inherent in the nature of the actual research tools developed since only certain forms of observational recording will be susceptible to qualitative or quantitative approaches. However, some forms of data gathering will be susceptible to both quantitative and qualitative methods or, even more commonly, will enable an interaction between methods. Alternatively, one research tool that employs observation may be employed as the concomitant of another element within a blended approach.

Researchers employing observational techniques must be extremely sensitive to ethical considerations since the process of observation may easily be confused with some form of onerous surveillance by the subject or subjects of observation. It is essential that all those involved in the research process are completely clear how the data derived from such methods will be employed and that there will be no question that such material will be used for other purposes such as appraisal or performance management.

Despite such complexities and challenges observation can be one of the most rewarding of research approaches. Although observation may, and has, formed the main research tool for major, funded research studies it can also be a particularly relevant method for small-scale research by the practitioner researcher.

FURTHER READING

◆ DeWalt, K. M. and DeWalt, B. R., *Participant Observation: A Guide for Fieldworkers*, London: Altamira (2001)

◆ Fine, G. A. and Sandstrom, K. L., *Knowing Children: Participant Observation with Minors (Qualitative Research Methods)*, London: Sage (1998)

◆ Hopkins, D., *A Teacher's Guide to Classroom Research*, Milton Keynes: Open University Press (2007)

◆ Montgommery, D., *Helping Teachers Develop Through Classroom Observation*, London: David Fulton (2002)

◆ Rodriguez, N. M. and Ryave, A. L., *Systematic Self-Observation: A Method for Researching the Hidden and Elusive Features of Everyday Social Life (Qualitative Research Methods)*, London: Sage (2002)

◆ Sharman, C., Vennis, D. and Cross, W., *Observing Children: A Practical Guide (Cassell Studies in Pastoral Care and Personal and Social Education)*, London: Continuum (1995)

How to Ask – Deciphering Documentation

By the conclusion of this chapter it is anticipated that you will:

◆ be able to recognise the strengths and weaknesses of documents and appreciate the appropriateness of the approach to support other formats; and
◆ be able to construct recording formats suitable to the contextual and conceptual foci of the research.

Documentation, in one form or another, is an essential source of information for a large proportion of research studies. However, you do need to be aware of the disagreements that exist between authors working in the field of education research methodology as to what actually constitutes 'documents' (in the context of research) and how they can be incorporated as a research methodology. Cohen *et al* (2007), for example, only include documentation as an element of a historical research approach, due mainly it is presumed, to the pre-existing nature of documents. This chapter attempts to establish the parameters of 'documentary evidence', the type of information that it can provide, identify the potential strengths and weaknesses, and provide an indication of how to construct recording formats to collect and collate evidence in this form.

What is a 'document'?

A fairly simple and straightforward question on the face of it, but inextricably linked to the context and focus of the research. In essence all sources which can be used as part of the evidence base for your research, but were not produced specifically for your research, can be classed as documents. This will include all forms of publication and recording including:

◆ printed materials (text and images);
◆ electronic media (text, images, audio and video); and
◆ artefacts (models, equipment, physical resources, etc).

Denscombe (2003), along with Cohen *et al* (2007) lists books and journals within their definition of 'documentary evidence'; indeed Denscombe (2003: 212) refers to it as the 'first port of call' for researchers, well it is, but not as a source of evidence. We feel that it is important to draw a clear line of distinction here between sources which inform the direction and content of the research and sources which *are* the research. The review of existing published literature on a specific theme – a 'literature review' of theory, conceptual frameworks and published empirical research – will be used by you to help you to construct your research activity, it will not *be* your research activity. In our view these sources deserve to be treated quite differently, hence our focus on this as 'reviewing existing ideas' (chapter 3). Structurally this then gives us:

◆ national/government publications – used to establish the national context;
◆ documents produced by the organisation – used to set the local context of the study; and
◆ books, journal articles (paper and electronic publication) and web-based articles (of appropriate providence) – used to establish the conceptual framework.

If any, it is those documents listed as 'contextual' that are more likely to be redesignated as 'evidence'. If the focus of your study is at the national policy level, then the documents produced by the various government offices will form a significant part of your evidence base. Similarly, if you are focusing on the (re)development of school policy, then these policies will be central to your research effort, rather than simply contextualising it.

After putting these 'distractions' to one side we can concentrate on an examination of those sources which provide evidence for your research but which were produced for other reasons. In many respects, the enormous increase in the levels of accountability within state-funded education over the past 25 years has resulted in the production of quite staggering quantities of documentation. At all stages of the education process, from pre-school to higher education, planning, assessment and evaluation, and much more, have to be recorded for various levels of inspection. All of this provides the researcher with a rich, if not confusingly excessive, potential source of data.

Evidence of learning, for example, can be obtained through a review of the written work or artefacts produced by the learners; the teacher assessment and feedback given to those submissions; the assessment records maintained by teachers; self-assessment/evaluation activities completed by the learners; reports and references written by teachers/tutors; plus a host of collated, statistical data from formal testing.

At a management level there are likely to be meeting minutes, memos, emails, policy documents, briefings, curriculum and syllabus documents, room and equipment booking sheets, risk assessment forms, job descriptions. Additionally there is also all of the documentation produced for public consumption such as brochures, web pages, newsletters and mission statements.

However, it is not just the educational organisations themselves that sup-ply documents, there are many supporting organisations, particularly given the broader educational agenda as a result of Every Child Matters, that also pro-duce paper and electronic-based documentation which might be of relevance to an education-based researcher. Included within this would be the material hosted at www.teachers.tv which has television programmes recording school and classroom-based activities.

To sum up then, with documents:

◆ The data already exists in a definitive form (for example, a diary that has already been written, independent of the research, is a document; one which has been commissioned for the purpose of this research; is an extended form of questionnaire).
◆ It cannot be individually designed to suit a particular research purpose.
◆ It must be drawn on as a source of data in the form in which it stands.
◆ It is an unobtrusive or non-reactive research tool.
◆ It is not affected by the fact that it is being used for research purposes.

How can documents be used in research activity?

As documents are a recording, in one format or another, of events, thoughts or perceptions, they represent a particular point in time. A lesson plan, for example, represents the *expectations* for learning and activities, not what actually *did* happen or was learnt. Similarly, an evaluation following a lesson is likely to be layered and effected by the perceptions of the person writing the evaluation. As such most documents offer a base-line against which other sources can be compared and contrasted.

Case Study 8.1 Evaluating the effect of giving written feedback to KS2 learners in a large primary school

New deputy headteacher (MA student) 'Nina'

Being new to the school when she was asked to perform this evaluation, Nina referred to the school's policy document on assessment to establish what was actually 'supposed' to be happening. This was then compared to what teachers thought that they were meant to be doing, what was actually being written in pupils' books (further documentary evidence) and, through interviews with the children, what impact it appeared to be having on their learning.

Policy documents, particularly in the case of classroom-based research, do offer a productive starting place as they provide a strong indication of what should be happening. Admittedly this does depend on the perspective from which the policy was written and how dated it is. Some policies are written to represent the current reality (or more likely, the best of current practice); whereas others might be more aspirational in their tone, giving an indication of what is being striven for rather than actually achieved. In either case, the documentary source provides a 'known point' against which evidence from other sources can be compared.

A lesson plan may provide an excellent foundation for an interview following an observation of that lesson. In particular it would provide the teacher with the opportunity to discuss and justify any divergences from the original plan.

Many teachers in the compulsory phases of education will adopt a similar process when faced with a class of relatively unknown children and a set of standardised test results achieved at the completion of the previous school year. The documentary evidence is accepted as a starting point, but is then modified as this is compared and contrasted with evidence from other (more current) sources, such as direct observation, interviewing (asking the learners pertinent questions) and subsequent documentary evidence (artefacts and other tangible 'work' completed by the learners).

Most documents offer a 'snapshot' in time, reflecting or capturing a particular reality. This offers not only the interviewer the opportunity to reanalyse the documents with changed perceptions following the passage of time, but also to identify and respond to change. Learning is all about change, so written work (or videoed interviews for another example) collected from learners before and after a 'learning opportunity', presents the researcher with a useful set of comparative data:

◆ concept maps showing children's ideas on a particular scientific concept before and after the use of a specific learning technique;
◆ video of a class of children before and after the teacher has applied and embedded a set of behaviour management techniques; and
◆ comparing the lesson plans produced by a PGCE trainee at the beginning and end of their course to compare the level of sophistication and pedagogic knowledge being demonstrated.

Going beyond those documents that are for the classroom-based researcher, many others support research into educational management issues.

Case Study 8.2 Establishing a vision for a new specialist sports college: analysing the competition

Assistant headteacher responsible for sports college status (MA student) 'Mike'

Having been charged with bringing a paper to the governing body concerning how the college should present itself 'renewed' to the community following its change of status, Mike chose to collect, collate and analyse documentary evidence from two distinct populations – local colleges (potential competitors) and existing sports colleges in other areas of the country. The source of the

Continued

documents were the websites of these colleges which were used to publicly declare their educational and organisational values and aims. From this Mike was able to offer suggestions that were consistent with many of the mission statements from the sports colleges, but made them distinct from other local schools.

Case Study 8.3 What are primary schools looking for when appointing new science subject leaders?

Primary BEd dissertation student 'Tim'

In an attempt to discover the extent to which the course he had attended for four years had been preparing him for the role, he used the 'jobs' section of *TES* to obtain the details for all promoted-post primary science subject leaders over a six-month period. He analysed the requirements in terms of science subject knowledge, leadership/management; skills/experience and general teaching skills/experience.

Educational establishments collect and retain a significant amount of information that is not directly concerned with learning and teaching – although much of it will have a substantial influence on it.

◆ Attendance records – are some days/times more 'popular' than others? (is Monday more poorly attended than any other day? For both staff and students!).

◆ Minutes of meetings – do different departments discuss similar issues? What proportion of meetings is actually spent on debate and decision making as opposed to information giving?

Documents are useful to the researcher, not only in terms of the content, but also in terms of the presentation (the style, language, format, etc). Documents are clearly meant to convey information – evidence that is presented 'wittingly'; but it may also be possible to extract information that the author did not knowingly include – 'unwitting' evidence. For example, the minutes of a meeting may not simply reflect what happened and who said what; the status of individuals may also be conveyed in the language (teachers being referred to by surname and teaching assistants by their first name). Different authors may adopt different styles for different types of document (for different audiences or purposes) and it is the researcher who needs to be aware of this and learn to 'read between the lines' and assess the significance.

In all of these examples given above, the researcher has to rely on others to produce the evidence that they will be using in their research. But just how reliable is it?

Assessing documents

As noted in chapter 3, that researchers need to assure themselves of the providence of the literature that they are using to base their conceptual arguments upon, you must also be sure of the validity and accuracy of the evidence you intend to collect from documents. In assessing the value of documentary evidence there are two levels at which you need to operate:

1. *External criticism* – conformation of the 'authenticity or genuineness' (Cohen *et al*, 2007:195) of the source.
2. *Internal criticism* – conformation of the value and accuracy of the content of the document (how credible is it?).

The first imperative is to confirm that the document is from a sound source (that is, not faked, forged or knowingly distorted) and is authentic. One researcher, examining the way that local KS2/3 schools risk assessed study trips into the local community to teach aspects of geography, found herself in receipt of risk assessments from eight schools – five of which were identical (complete with a spelling mistake) other than date, school name and the signatory! Whilst it is quite frequent to find that policies, curricula and certain other documentation has been 'based' on those used in other institutions and suitably adapted and amended prior to adoption, there have been cases where the adoption has taken placed with only perfunctory levels of engagement, which really questions their validity if not rightful ownership.

Credibility can be a problem with certain documents in education, particularly those written for more than one purpose. Lesson plans and evaluations may be written more for the mentor or tutor than the teacher and so may not accurately represent what the teacher intends, or is able, to deliver. Similarly, departmental minutes may be written knowing that senior management are expecting certain issues to be discussed and so minutes will reflect expectations rather than reality.

Sampling is a particular issue with documentation. As Denscombe (2003:220) asks 'is the document typical of its type?' Choice may be restricted by access – you may only be offered those lesson plans, for example, that respondents feel 'confident' with – the best examples, rather than those with are more representative of the general level of quality.

Given that documentation is often written with the expectation that it will only be viewed by an internal audience, accurate interpretation can require significant levels of 'insider knowledge'. It may not just be a matter of the language and possible codes used, but also what could be implied and what is omitted. Interpretation by the author or someone with the requisite 'insider knowledge' may be required to bridge potential gaps between the intended meaning and the received meaning.

Above all else, the key determinant in assessing the values of a document must be 'does it help me with my research?', specifically 'does it help me to answer my questions?' If not, it should be rejected as a source of evidence.

Accessing documents

Ethically, you need to inform your potential research population of the purpose of your research when you request information from them. As suggested above, this may significantly impact on the willingness of your potential respondents to participate – or it may at least mean that you are presented with a 'selection' of the documentation or an edited version of it. It is possible that you have access to the documentation, but not for this particular purpose. For example, as head of a cohort or subject area within your organisation you may have access, in your professional capacity, to all planning, curriculum schemes, assessment feedback and so on, produced by your team. However, if you are also using the documentation, which you are examining and analysing for professional purposes, as an evidence base for an assignment towards an academic award, you will need to discuss your position with your tutor to clarify your position and that of the evidence. Clearly your relationship, particularly the level of trust, with the research population will have a significant impact on this process.

To gain access to documentary sources that would not normally be within your reach (a different organisation or even department), you would be advised to work through a member of the senior management team who will have access. As suggested in the first section to this book, to ensure that your research effort is welcomed, it is worth working with a senior manager from the very earliest of stages so that they can act as your 'gatekeeper'.

Developing documentary research tools

The development of research tools specific for documents is dependent upon the research paradigm that is being adopted. The interpretive model would suggest that researchers would adopt an approach which would immerse themselves in the data to begin the search for what is important. This approach is frequently used in the early stages of a research activity to get the 'feel' for the nature and scope of the issues that need to be addressed through the research activity, in much the same way that you might have a preliminary 'chat' with colleagues to discover if they have the same perceptions of a 'problem' as you. The positivist researcher would clarify what they are seeking from the evidence base and focus upon that. Interpretism may appear to be the 'easy option' but the data can quickly become overwhelming. Positivism may mean that many 'interesting' points found in the evidence must be disregarded as irrelevant, but it can make the whole process more manageable and focused. Pragmatically, it would be prudent, when adopting a positivist approach, to maintain an explicit focus, but make a note of any 'interesting' points of information that arise out of the data collection.

Robson (2002) suggests that the whole process is broken down as:

◆ start with a research question;
◆ decide on a sampling strategy;
◆ define the recording unit;
◆ construct categories for analysis;
◆ test the coding on samples of text and assess reliability; and
◆ carry out the analysis.

Robson uses the research question as an anchor with the conceptual literature being implicit in the identification and construction of the 'recording units' and 'categories for analysis'.

In the same way that interview and observation schedules ensure that the researcher maintains a focus which is consistent with the aims of the research, so documents must be treated the same way. As the documents will not have been constructed for the purpose of the research that you are carrying out, you can maintain your focus much more successfully by constructing a research tool which will keep you on track. As with interview schedules and questionnaires (see chapter 6), it can be helpful to construct your research tool in three sections:

◆ *Biographical* – information about the document (for example, authorship, title/identifier, age, source).
◆ *Factual* – information that you wish to gain from the source (from your conceptual reading, based upon the focus from the research question), both witting and unwitting.
◆ *Opinion* – your (as the researcher) informed opinion of the validity and reliability of the source and any additional witting and unwitting evidence to be gleaned from it.

Case Study 8.4 Data collection schedule for (science subject leader)

Biographical details: Name of school ....

| Date of advert | applications by | interview date |
| Size of school | authority | salary point |

Information sent: job description ☐   school brochure ☐   job/person spec. ☐

Application form ☐   other ....

Factual:	essential (numbers)	desirable (numbers)
Science	☐	☐
Management	☐	☐
Teaching	☐	☐
Other	☐	☐

Specific statements ....

Continued

Opinion:

Job specification style and structure ...

Language used ....

Personalisation ...

Other....

The schedule, constructed to collect and collate information sent out by primary schools seeking to appoint a science subject leader, is designed to offer the researcher a consistent format for comparing the documentation. A separate schedule is completed for each set of documentation, in much the same way that individual respondents complete questionnaires. Inevitably there is an element of interpretation of the documentation as the schedule is completed, which brings in the potential of researcher bias, but with a single researcher it would be hoped that any bias would be acknowledged – and at least be consistent!

The factual element of the schedule seeks to identify key terms or phrases within the documentation and record them quantitatively. This 'content analysis' will need to link directly back to the key ideas identified in your examination of the conceptual and empirical literature.

Research tip

Photocopy the original document and then, using a selection of different coloured highlighter pens for the different categories, mark the key points and tally them.

If the document is in an electronic format; scanning with optical character recognition (OCR) software will be effective; then there are various software packages available that will find the key terms for you – if you tell it what to look for. Microsoft's MsWord will even do this in a limited way using the *Edit-Find-Highlight* option.

Content analysis can be used for many purposes:

◆ sentence length in text books (as an indication of readability);
◆ 'ethnicity' of names in reading books;
◆ positive/negative language in reports and student feedback;
◆ suitability of websites; and
◆ use of behaviour management techniques used in exemplar lessons (on video) for training purposes.

An interesting example using an analysis of images involved a student exploring how universities encourage 'widening participation' through the images used in their undergraduate prospectuses (that is, 'older' or non-white students). One university scored a high 'black-male' count; unfortunately it was often the same black-male student, who appeared to be on several different courses across all faculties!

Case Study 8.5 To what extent are maths teachers planning lessons to meet the needs of all their students?

Head of Maths in a large secondary school (MA student) 'Jude'

As part of a year long initiative to help teachers in the department become more responsive to the learning needs of the students Jude wanted to supplement the observations of lessons with an examination of a sample of lesson planning.

Biographical details: Name of teacher ....

| Date of lesson | topic | time | day |
| Year | group | support? | |

Factual:

| Objectives | knowledge ☐ | skills ☐ | differentiated ☐ |
| Phases | intro ☐ | activity ☐ | plenary ☐ |

Continued

Teaching	VAK ☐	group ☐	whole class ☐
	Timings ☐	Key questions ☐	resources ☐

Other content ....

Opinion:

Lesson plan style and structure ...

Language used ....

Evaluation ...

Case Study 8.6 Student learning through MsPowerpoint presentations – are tutors making effective use of the medium?

Learning 'advocate' in an FE college (MA student) 'Krish'

Tutors at the college were increasing making use of this presentation format which they were placing on the college's VLE to allow the students further access and allow them to print off handouts prior to sessions. But were the tutors aware of the best ways to use the format? A sample of presentations were downloaded from the VLE and analysed.

Biographical details: Name of tutor.................

Course	subject	year group

Factual:

Presentation	background colour(s) ☐	style ☐
	title font ☐ size ☐	colour ☐
	text font ☐ size ☐	colour ☐
Transition	slide ☐ elements ☐	

Continued

Content word density ☐ graphics ☐ objectives ☐

session length ☐ number of slides ☐

Opinion:

Presentation colour scheme ...

Language used ....

Embedded notes ...

In each case, it is helpful to consider each document as a 'respondent' who is providing information for your research and to help you keep to your focus, the schedule will be invaluable.

Analysing documentary evidence

This is different from assessing the validity and reliability of the documents themselves (a particular focus for many research methodology texts) and relates purely to the evidence that you have collected from the documents.

Content analysis has already been referred to above and, as suggested, can be of both quantitative and qualitative form. In this respect, it is little different from evidence collected by any other means. Textual documentary analysis does offer a particular form of detailed analysis not open to other formats – even a transcript of an interview cannot adequately account for the facial expression, body language, or even vocal inflection (in the particular case of non-face-to-face interviews) that will have been an integral element of the communication within the interview. Linguistic analyses of written text can become incredibly detailed and self-involved; in most situations, the research that you will be performing will be focusing on the extent to which the language (word and structure) adequately conveys meaning to the intended audience.

As suggested above, there is an element of analysis through selection within the data collection process (note-taking in an interview or observation is similar in this respect).

Finally, expanding upon the pros and cons of using documentary evidence given in chapter 5.

Summary of strengths

1. It is an unobtrusive method (when you don't have to ask to gain access).
2. You can collect data without being observed (be aware of ethical considerations).
3. The data are in permanent form and can be subject to reanalysis, allowing reliability checks (as long as you have stored and organised it).
4. It may provide a low cost form of longitudinal analysis (where the same data is collected over time).
5. Enables enquiry into past events where there is no access to contemporary participants (validity and reliability may be hard to check).
6. May help to triangulate other evidence (offers a good base line).

And weaknesses

1. The documents available may be limited or partial (try to find out why it is incomplete).
2. The documents have been written for purposes unconnected with the research and may be biased or distorted (examine rationale of author).
3. Documents are not neutral reports and may be shaped by the context and the assumptions of participants (examine rationale of author).
4. The documents may not be credible, authentic or representative.

FURTHER READING

◆ Cohen, L., Manion, L. and Morrison, K., *Research Methods in Education* (6th Ed) Abingdon: Routledge (2007)

◆ Duffy, B., 'The Analysis of Documentary Evidence', in Bell, J., *Doing your Research Project* Buckingham: Open University Press (2005)

◆ Fitzgerald, T., 'Documents and Documentary Analysis: reading between the lines in Briggs', A. J. R. and Coleman, M. (Eds) *Research Methods in Educational Leadership and Management* (2nd Ed) London: Sage Publications (2007)

◆ Hitchcock, G. and Hughes, D., *Research and the Teacher* (2nd Ed) Abingdon: Routledge (1995)

◆ Walliman, N., *Your Research Project*, London: Sage Publications (2005)

How to Ask – Action Research

The closeness of action research to 'reflective practice' is both a strength and a drawback for the educational professional, so it is important that by the end of this chapter your will have had the opportunity to:

◆ recognise the strengths and weaknesses of action research and its relationship to 'reflective practice'; and
◆ construct an appropriate action research strategy suitable to the research context and the conceptual focus.

Introduction

In the previous three chapters there has been a degree of detachment between the researcher and the research context to encourage an objective research perspective. Action research, as an approach, encourages a use of mixed methods, an objective research perspective, combined with active intervention. As with a series of connected lessons – subsequent lessons being shaped by the outcomes from previous sessions – action research employs an iterative research process to steer an initiative towards a desired outcome, with each iteration being informed and directed by an analysis of the evidence gathered in respect of a further consideration of the conceptual literature and comparable published research findings.

For example, challenging the current belief that use of the modern foreign language (MFL) must predominate in the MFL classroom, a teacher of modern foreign languages may wish to explore whether the use of English for the explanation and clarification of grammar points can result in increased learner engagement and improved learning outcomes across the entire ability range. A Year 7 Science teacher may be aware of the disparity of pupils' learning experiences in primary education and would like to investigate how this affects their progression and attainment at KS3. In collaboration with colleagues from primary feeder schools s/he would like to develop, implement and evaluate a transition intervention programme, which has the aim of bridging the perceived gap between the primary and secondary curriculum and facilitate smooth progression from KS2 to KS3 for all children.

The nature of 'action research'

In order to shed light on a particular situation in relation to which you have identified issues that need addressing you may consider undertaking an action research project, either on your own or in collaboration with colleagues. The processes involved in such an enquiry are not dissimilar to those informing teachers' production of an end of year report. Any judgements or evaluations of pupil performance must be evidence-based, but will also include supplementary information that has emerged outside the formal assessment procedure. It can include both formative and summative elements and should be guided by two concepts: assessment *for* learning and assessment *of* learning. Similarly, action research generates findings *for* practice (informing practice) as well as *of* practice (research report). In both cases the process of evidence gathering will be positioned within temporal, conceptual and thematic boundaries, which provides a clear focus and enhances the validity of findings.

As in teaching, where the assessment of pupil learning will be conducted via a specific set of activities (for example, written test, practical task, coursework, homework, classwork), action researchers need to select their methods for data collection carefully, taking into consideration the nature of the enquiry and participants involved. For example, by adopting a quantitative approach, non-participant observation would suggest itself as a possible strategy with the aim of obtaining an objective view of teacher and pupil behaviour in the classroom. In order to elucidate the behaviour patterns observed and examine the underlying motives, a qualitative approach by means of in-depth one-to-one interviews or learning journals would be appropriate.

Practitioner action research is commonly associated with the concept of 'reflective practice' (Schön, 1983; 1987), a process within which reflection can be triggered by

the recognition that in some respects a situation is in need of special attention'
(Eraut, 1984:144). Most teachers engage in this process regularly in their day-
to-day practice when they reflect on how a particular group of pupils responds
to a new teaching approach, learning strategy or resource and whether this new
idea requires further modification, should be retained or abandoned. Sometimes,
such reflection manifests itself in reflective dialogues and may even provoke action
within a department or across the whole school. Although teacher reflection is
often followed by action, and action is followed by reflection, the generation of
so-called evidence is often anecdotal and derived from *ad hoc* experiences. Like
any other form of research, practitioner action research needs to satisfy a set of
quality criteria by ensuring that the process reflects a rigorous and systematic
approach. As such it needs to go beyond practice with a focus on knowledge that
informs action rather than the action itself and is concerned with practitioners' values, beliefs and motives and how these influence them in their actions (McNiff,
1996). The action cycle starts with an issue or a problem that has been identified in a certain situation (classroom or school as a whole) and that is in need of
resolving through an intervention programme, a new strategy or the implementation of a new framework, policy or procedure. Practitioner action research is
thus 'insider' research, which can provide teachers with a framework for enquiry
into their professional practices. It can enable them to engage in critical reflection about issues related to their own and other practice settings in a systematic
manner.

Practitioner-based action research can be conducted at different levels of critical
engagement reflecting a technical, practical and emancipatory focus (Kemmis &
McTaggart, 1992; McKernan, 1991; Zuber-Skerritt, 1996). It can be used to find solutions to technical problems, without questioning the legitimacy of these techniques
or the framework within which they are to be applied. Effective implementation of the literacy hour springs to mind. Where the focus of action research
is practical it takes into account social and cultural factors inherent in the setting and how they might affect learning. For example, the problem of truancy
may not be effectively addressed by taking a harsher stance in terms of sanc-
tions, but may require action and enquiry that incorporates a range of perspectives
(pupils, parents/carers, teachers, children services). By allowing those at the heart
of the process a voice, it would also reflect an emancipatory agenda (Groundwater-
Smith & Mockler, 2007), the core aims of which are empowerment of individuals
and social groups that have been marginalised and whose voices need to be
heard.

Definition of action research

During the past 15 years or so, action research has enjoyed immense popularity amongst practitioners in education and other professional fields, such as health, business and management. Its potential contributions to improving professional practice through critical enquiry and reflection have been brought to the fore in recent literature on teachers' CPD and school improvement (Campbell *et al*, 2004; Dadds, 1995; Dadds & Hart, 2001; Burton & Bartlett, 2005). Although action research takes a variety of forms, its key features manifest themselves in how researchers and research participants relate to and interact with each other and how knowledge is constructed. Unlike conventional scientific research the philosophy underpinning this research genre reflects a strong democratic dimension (Carr & Kemmis, 1986), in that it often includes 'service users' (pupils, parents/carers) in the research process (Beresford, 1999; Winter & Munn-Giddings, 2001) and seeks to give voice to those who are 'culturally silenced' (Winter, 1998).

In Education, the term 'action research' has become a key ingredient in the discourses concerned with the improvement and development of professional practice from within the profession, implying notions of ownership and participation in the generation of new insights into processes of teaching and learning. According to Kemmis and McTaggart (1982) 'action research is the way in which groups of people can organise the conditions under which they can learn from their own experience, and make this experience accessible to others' (1988: 7), or as Waterman describes it:

> 'to make improvements ... by working with the organisational actors in a cycle of action, data gathering, analysis, reflection and planning further action, as the researchers and the organisation work together. Praxis and research go together, each taking account of the other, and influencing the way people think about an issue' (2000: 495).

In this sense action research is frequently employed to address issues arising from professional practice with the aim of constructing knowledge collaboratively in order to bring about change and improvement (Lewin, 1952; Carr & Kemmis, 1986; Elliott, 1991). It thus promotes ownership of the research process by those who will be most affected by its outcomes with the predominant aim 'to improve practice rather than to produce knowledge' (Elliott, 1991: 49). The key principle underpinning such research could be described as essentially democratic in that it implies the active participation of practitioners in the research process with the aim of trying to change practice and as such its success 'will depend, in large measure, on [...] success with working with other people' (Gray, 2004: 377). It can be conducted by individuals or a group of practitioners, who have identified an area in their professional practice that they consider in need of further development of improvement. Working with fellow practitioners and peers, however, requires a sensitive approach towards and respect for others' feelings and expertise in the field. In this respect it is important to highlight the strong philosophical underpinning in terms of the ethical/moral principles inherent in action research and how they are reflected in the four outcomes identified by McNiff *et al* (1996: 8):

◆ personal development;
◆ improved professional practice;
◆ improvements in the institution in which you work; and
◆ contribution to the good order of society.

Traditionally, though, insider action research is concerned with institutional improvement, development of practice and organisational learning and involves practitioners with a leadership or management role. McNiff highlights the point that when you undertake your own action research, you need to put the 'I' at the centre (1996:17), which needs to go along with an explanation of how you are positioned in relation to the research setting and other research participants. More recently, action research increasingly involves the active participation of pupils, without whose views, opinions and experiences many questions posed by teachers would remain unanswered. The inclusion of children's voices form an integral element in participatory action research (PAR), which has as its primary aim to transform situations and structures in an egalitarian manner (Gray, 2004:375). But most importantly, your decision to choose an action research design must arise directly from the focus of your enquiry.

Identifying the general idea

As mentioned earlier, the general idea around which the research is to be constructed needs to relate to a situation which is deemed to be in need of improvement or change. This mirrors the teaching and learning situation, in which teachers recognise a discrete area in their pupils' cognitive and socio-emotional development or, indeed, in their own behaviour as teachers, which requires targeted action. The following examples illustrate how such 'general ideas' are derived from situations that are perceived to require action:

9.1 Starting points

Example A:

Students have expressed dissatisfaction with an overemphasis on the use of text-based resources in history, which they find boring and are not related to reality. How can they, and their teacher, collaboratively explore a more diverse way of teaching and learning?

Example B:

Year heads have become aware of the fact that absenteeism amongst Year 7 pupils has increased dramatically. How can they reverse this trend by investigating the underlying causes in collaboration with pupils, parents/carers and secondary and primary colleagues and respond to pupil needs after transfer from primary to secondary school?

Example C:

A teacher has become aware of a marked discrepancy between the quality of students' work in class and their homework, which is consistently of poor quality. How can she ensure that students' independent work at home is of a similar quality to that produced in class?

When considering your area for action research, it is helpful to take cognisance of Elliott's (1991: 72) caveat. First, you need to ensure that the general idea is related to your field of action, that the situation you intend to change or improve is in need of such action and that the extent to which this can be achieved must not be based on your assumptions but be the result of the action research. You must, therefore, be prepared for unexpected findings to emerge, which may necessitate the revision of your original general idea.

Formulating the research question

As a teacher you are only too aware of the importance of careful preparation and planning of lessons in your endeavour to assist students in achieving the intended learning outcomes. This situation resonates with Lewin's (1946) notion of 'recon naissance', which precedes any action research by finding out more about the particular situation you have identified in need of improvement. If we return to the three examples given earlier the fact finding mission may include questions like the following:

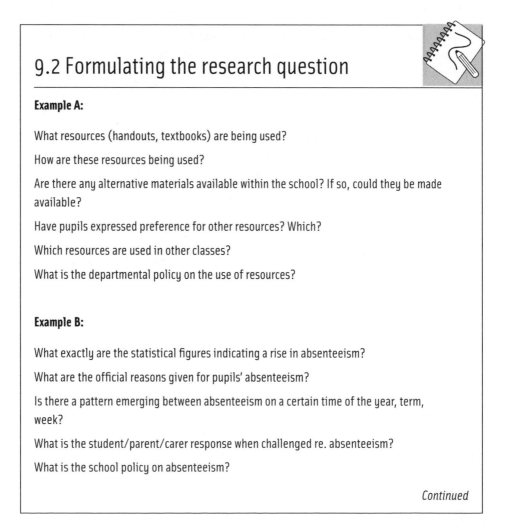

9.2 Formulating the research question

Example A:

What resources (handouts, textbooks) are being used?

How are these resources being used?

Are there any alternative materials available within the school? If so, could they be made available?

Have pupils expressed preference for other resources? Which?

Which resources are used in other classes?

What is the departmental policy on the use of resources?

Example B:

What exactly are the statistical figures indicating a rise in absenteeism?

What are the official reasons given for pupils' absenteeism?

Is there a pattern emerging between absenteeism on a certain time of the year, term, week?

What is the student/parent/carer response when challenged re. absenteeism?

What is the school policy on absenteeism?

Continued

Example C:

What is the school's/department's homework policy?

How is feedback communicated to the pupils and parents/carers?

To what extent do pupils and parents/carers take an active role in the monitoring and evaluation of homework?

These questions can inform the formulation of the research questions to be addressed and provide a basic structure around which to plan and conduct the actions. They can also give an indication of possible categories for the collection and analysis of data. By developing a catalogue of questions, initial assumptions may be dispersed in the light of the findings, resulting in a new interpretation of the situation to be investigated. Subsequently, the revised perception can but need not lead to a hypothesis, which according to Elliott describes 'the situation', indicates a need for improvement or change and explains the relationship between the two.

9.3 Stating the hypothesis

Example A:

A multi-sensory approach to teaching and learning can enhance pupils' learning experience and result in improved learning outcomes.

Example B:

The active involvement of pupils and parents/carers is a crucial element in a strategy to combat rising exclusion rates.

Example C:

The quality of homework can be improved through a feedback dialogue involving pupils, parents/carers and the teacher.

Such a hypothesis is not to be understood in the strictly scientific/positivistic sense, which is either proved or disproved in the form of measurable quantitative data. Instead, it is to be perceived as a device to frame a critical enquiry into professional practice with the aim of gaining new insights into processes the efficacy of which remained unquestioned previously, and to acquire a more profound understanding of the various, complex factors influencing the teaching and learning process.

The action research process

In their day-to-day practice, theoretical perspectives of teaching and learning may not be at the forefront of teachers' thinking and doing, although occasional reference to pedagogical models can be helpful in justifying or questioning certain practices. Similarly, action research is primarily about 'action', although theoretical perspectives can provide a helpful framework for the research design in terms of the structure of the research process. We will now consider some action research models as presented in the literature.

Kurt Lewin (1952), a social psychologist, conceived the action research process as consisting of a 'spiral of cycles', which start with a general idea, followed by fact finding (reconnaissance) and subsequent planning of action. After developing and implementing the first action step evaluation takes place, which informs the revision of the original plan. This model was refined further by Kemmis (1980), Elliott (1991) and Carr and Kemmis (1986) and can be translated into a more concrete timetable format, specifying the duration of the action and clearly stating start and finish and the type of activities employed for data collection and evaluation. For example, Carr and Kemmis (1986:165) describe the action research process as 'a spiral of cycles of planning, acting, observing and reflecting, with each of these activities being systematically and self-critically implemented and interrelated'. As illustrated in Figure 9.1, the insights gained from one cycle will subsequently be used to formulate the new need for change and the planning of the action of the next cycle.

The various models presented in the literature suggest that action research is a neat process made up of logically sequenced stages of activities. However, it can be a 'messy business' (Cook, 1998), which manifests itself in u-turns, cul-de-sacs,

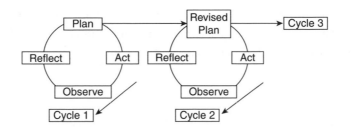

Fig. 9.1 ◆ Action research cycles

off-shoots of new, emerging issues, which may also be worth pursuing, but which would detract from the original focus of the enquiry. The following model provides a possible mapping and sequencing of discrete activities, as they may occur in an action research cycle (Fig. 9.2):

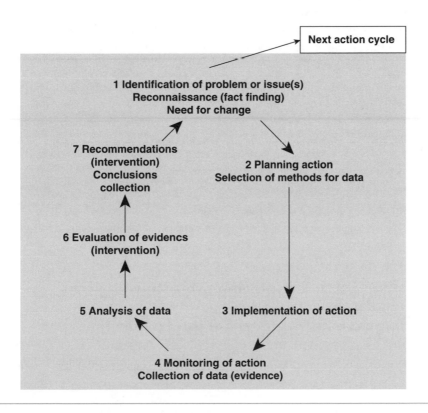

Fig. 9.2 ◆ Activities inherent in an action cycle

Moving from an abstract model to its practical application in the 'real world' is not always straight forward. To help you make the connection, we would like you to consider Scenarios 9.1 and 9.2 and associated questions.

Scenario 9.1: Improving pupil behaviour and learner engagement

As a class teacher of a Year 3 (primary) you would like to administer an intervention to achieve improvements in pupil behaviour and learner engagement. You have identified a number of strategies which you would like to trial:

- rigorous monitoring of disruptions and identification of causes (for example, gold/silver/ colour stars on 'star chart');
- introduction of individual and collective reward system for good behaviour, effort and achievement (for example, 'golden' hour once a month when pupils can choose an activity they would like to do); and
- introduce element of pupil ownership by developing a catalogue classroom rules (to be agreed with pupils and to be displayed on the classroom wall).

Questions:

1. How many action cycles would you include?
2. What would be the duration of each cycle?
3. What would be the start and finish of each cycle?

Scenario 9.2: Facilitating opportunities for CPD through a mentoring/coaching framework

You are the assistant head of a secondary school with responsibility for staff development and performance management. In order to develop greater coherence between these two aspects,

Continued

the senior management team has decided to introduce a mentoring/coaching framework for all teaching and support staff within the school. You are unsure as to what extent this new framework will provide opportunities for teachers' professional learning and development in a structure/unstructured, formal/informal environment. You have, therefore, decided to run a pilot over a 12-month period.

Questions:

1. How many action cycles would you include?
2. What would be the duration of each cycle?
3. What would be the start and finish of each cycle?
4. What activities would you select for the collection of data and who would be your participants? Please give reasons for your decision.
5. How would you sequence the activities? Please give reasons for your decision.

Planning your action research project

Although not immediately apparent, on closer examination of teachers' practice and action research, a number of parallel processes and activities become apparent. What they have in common is the systematic and coherent way in which they are constructed around a focus of the enquiry. Table 9.1 serves to make the links between teaching and action research more explicit:

Table 9.1 ◆ Links between teaching and action research

Teaching	Action research
Topic of teaching unit or scheme of work	Focus of action enquiry (the issue, the problem)
Number of specific lessons	Number of action cycles
Resources required to teach the unit	Resources required to gather evidence
Identification of teacher and learner activities	Identification of researcher and participant activities
Nature of relationship between teacher and learner and how this affects the learning process	Positionality of the research and how this affects the behaviour of other research participants

Continued

Table 9.1 ◆ Cont'd

Teaching	Action research
Ethical considerations: ◆ confidentiality of information; and ◆ balancing need for information and pupil's right to privacy.	Ethical considerations: ◆ balance of power and control; ◆ anonymity of participants; ◆ confidentiality of information; and ◆ gaining informed consent.
Selection of appropriate teaching/learning/assessment approach and strategies	Selection of appropriate research approach and strategies (quantitative/qualitative/mixed methodology)
Validity and reliability of assessment	Validity and trustworthiness of research findings
Multi-method approach in the generation of evidence for assessment	'Multi-technique' (Elliott, 1991:77), triangulation by method, data, perspective, site
Awareness of structural, social, cultural factors inherent in the teaching/learning environment and their impact on the teaching/learning process	Identification of potential methodological, epistemological, ethical issues and their impact on the quality of the research
Monitoring of learners' behaviour, attitude and critical incidents Gathering of evidence of learning: ◆ formal and informal; and ◆ formative and summative.	Data collection (quantitative and qualitative), including use of 'analytic memos' (Elliott, 1991) to assist in the interpretation of data and to inform the next cycle.
Evidence of learning outcomes (marks and narrative report)	Research evidence (quantitative and qualitative data)
Analysis and interpretation of assessment data	Analysis and interpretation of research data
Conclusions drawn with regard to informing teaching and learning strategies	Conclusions drawn with regard to informing professional practice

Action research – a constructivist approach to knowledge creation

According to Capobianco & Feldman it is through the construction of knowledge and understanding that quality in action research is achieved (2006: 499), particularly so, as this process takes place within teachers' practice setting and is informed by the personal and professional perspectives of participants in a social constructivist manner. From our experience as project leaders of collaborative research projects we share this belief, but would also like to emphasise the need for a set of conditions that have to be met. First, collaborative action research in particular must reflect the principles underpinning Wenger's (1998) concept of a community of practice and those informing the practices of a knowledge-producing, epistemic community (Creplet *et al*, 2003). Accordingly, the members of an action research team must share a common goal, demonstrate a mutual commitment to the critical enquiry of a particular issue, problem or situation and share a repertoire of ideas and conceptualisations. Practitioner researchers, therefore, need to possess a thorough grounding in the nature of action research as well as knowledge of appropriate research methods (2006: 502). As I have learnt from my own experience as an action research project leader, achieving a high level of coherence in terms of shared understandings across all members of an action research team can be problematic, particularly where aspects of multi-disciplinary and multi-agency work is concerned. For example, action research located within the Every Child Matters agenda is highly likely to involve not only the perspectives of teachers and teaching assistants, but may also rely on contributions from other professional disciplines, such as social services, the police, health, psychology and counselling. In an attempt to identify potential challenges involved in multi-disciplinary research we would like you to consider Scenario 9.3 and associated questions.

Scenario 9.3

You are the head of a primary school, where the issue of child obesity has been identified as a problem that needs addressing. You intend to implement an intervention programme and evaluate its effectiveness via an action research approach. The outcome of the research will be used to inform curriculum development and school-parent partnerships with the aim of educating children towards a healthier life style.

Question:

Whose professional knowledge, experience and expertise could you draw upon in the implementation of an intervention, its evaluation and subsequent curriculum development?

Devise a multi-disciplinary team and explain the reasons for your decision.

Whilst diversity of perspectives and professional expertise is a prerequisite for devising a well-informed programme, it can pose enormous challenges for the research co-ordinator to maintain a certain degree of coherence and consensus amongst all participants. Troyna highlighted this issue when he stated that 'all research, from its conception through to the production of data, its interpretation and dissemination of findings reflects a partisanship which derives from the social identity and values of the researcher' (1995: 403). In addition participants will have vested interests and work within agendas, which are not always compatible.

Reporting your action research

One of the definitions of research includes the requirement that it is made public (Stenhouse, 1975). Within this remit the dissemination of action research outcomes can serve a range of purposes and may be presented in different ways. A teacher's findings may be used within a small circle of colleagues, who have agreed to share their experiences and evaluations of particular aspects of their professional practice. A wider audience may be involved, if the outcome of an action research project relates to whole school improvement (headteacher, governors) or is of interest to other, external agencies, such as Ofsted and LA advisers. Even if the report is to be disseminated in the public domain by means of conference presentation or publication of a journal article, the goal of action research would ultimately be to have an impact on professional practice, be it within a teacher's classroom, across departments or across several schools, in the way in which professional practice is reviewed, analysed and reassessed.

Caveats

In this chapter we have attempted to gain an understanding of action research, as a strategy of practice-based enquiry with the aim of improving practice. We considered the theoretical perspectives underpinning action research and investigated some of the potential methodological and ethical issues as they can arise in practice-based settings. It has become apparent that the processes involved in action research are not too dissimilar to those inherent in teaching and should, therefore, come naturally to any education practitioner who is committed to critical investigation and improvement of practice. However, whilst as a teacher you exercise a certain degree of control over the teaching, learning and assessment process, action research may not present itself as the neatly prescribed route you outlined in your project plan. It does not always progress in a linear fashion, but as highlighted by Dickens and Watkins (1999) can disperse in different directions, including reverse. It would, therefore, be foolish to suggest that such an undertaking is devoid of risks and pitfalls. To help you navigate your way through your action research project we would like you to take cognisance of the following caveats.

1. Be realistic in terms of the scope of your project and what can be achieved in a given amount of time in a particular practice setting.
2. In collaborative ventures, be aware of individuals' vested interests and different agendas.
3. Maintain positive relationships with all participants at all times.
4. Ensure transparency of the research process through effective communication with all parties involved.
5. Keep a detailed log of the research process.
6. Never apportion blame when things go wrong.
7. Be prepared to consider the views of others.
8. Appreciate the fact that teachers are busy professionals and cannot always give of their time.
9. Be flexible and be prepared for the unexpected.
10. Don't expect to find answers, be prepared to ask new questions.

Finally, we should take note of the warning sounded by Coghlan and Brannick's (2001). It is particularly relevant in school-based action research, where for example the implementation of policy and curriculum innovation can generate tensions amongst the various staff affected in terms of internal politics. In such situations action research can be perceived differently by the various stakeholders and even be misconstrued as subversive. It is, therefore, important to produce regular update reports to ensure that everybody is still in the loop of action.

FURTHER READING

◆ Burton, D. M. and Bartlett, S., *Practitioner Research for Teachers*, London: Sage (2005)

◆ Campbell, A., McNamara, O. and Gilroy, P., *Practitioner Research and Professional Development in Education*, London: Sage (2004)

◆ Elliott, J., *Action Research for Educational Change*, Buckingham: Open University Press (1991)

◆ Gray, D. E., *Doing Research in the Real World*, London: Sage (2004)

◆ McNiff, J., Lomaz, P. and Whitehead, J., *You and Your Action Research Project,* London: Routledge (1996)

Section 3
Reporting – Making Sense
of the Outcomes

This final section will guide you towards making the most effective use of the evidence that you have gathered. To ensure that you address the purposes that your research started out with, you will be given guidance on structuring the presentation and analysis of your findings, both qualitative and quantitative, and how to make an impact with the final conclusion and recommendations to be drawn from your study.

Presenting Your Findings

By the end of the chapter, you should:

◆ be able to appreciate the need to structure the presentation of the findings to address the initial purpose of the research; and
◆ be able to determine the most effective means of presenting different forms of data.

It is important to read this chapter in conjunction with the one that follows it; whilst it is possible to separate the presentation and analysis of your findings, it is essential that there is a consistency and internal integrity between them. It is through your selection, presentation and analysis of your findings that you will be able to demonstrate your true academic abilities. This chapter will consequently focus upon the processes involved in selecting key information from the evidence you have collected and using appropriate forms, including graphical and tabular, to clarify the findings to support the analysis and interpretation of your research outcomes.

Relationship between data presentation, data analysis and initial research questions

The whole purpose of completing the research activity is to address the research questions that were established in the introduction to your study so, in terms of effectiveness and efficiency, combining these elements offers a systematic approach. However, it may be necessary to structure these elements to the requirements of the format you are expected to write to. There are two formats which are most frequently adopted for the presentation and analysis of research data:

Example 10.1 – The 'atomistic' approach

Data presentation and analysis are separated.

Presentation

Data from each source are presented separately (often adopting a 'question by question' structure). For example:

Questionnaire responses (from the teaching staff in the school)

Interview responses (from the senior management team)

Documentary sources (school policy documents, meeting minutes, etc).

There is limited opportunity for interaction and comparison between the sources.

Analysis

The initial research questions are used as a structural device with data being reintroduced to support the analytical processes. For example: First research question: *'What are the key issues surrounding the management of behaviour?'* – relevant data from policy documents, teaching staff and managers are compared and then related to past research findings and theoretical perspectives from the literature.

Other research questions are addressed similarly.

Example 10.2 – The 'holistic' approach

Data presentation and analysis are combined.

Presentation with analysis

The initial research questions are used as a structural device with data being reintroduced to support the analytical processes. For example: First research question: *'What are the key issues*

Continued

surrounding the management of behaviour?' – relevant data from policy documents, teaching staff and managers are presented and compared and then related to past research findings and theoretical perspectives from the literature.

Subsequent research questions are addressed in the same way.

The way in which the data are brought to bear of the initial research questions will be crucial in the success of the study. If we look at the questions and sources of data given in the example (Fig. 10.1) a matching exercise can be performed.

Given that evidence from different sources needs to be presented to address each initial research question it is important that:

1. You have asked and collected the evidence in the first place!
2. You have identified which evidence from each source will be used to address each of the initial research questions.
3. You present the evidence in a coherent and explicit format which will allow for a clear analysis.

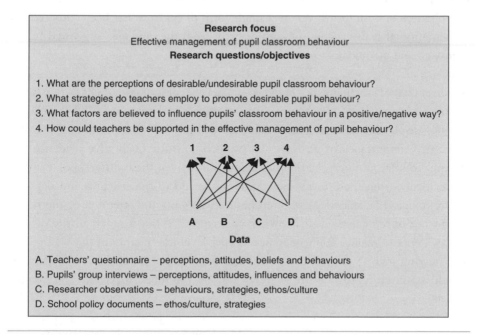

Research focus
Effective management of pupil classroom behaviour
Research questions/objectives

1. What are the perceptions of desirable/undesirable pupil classroom behaviour?
2. What strategies do teachers employ to promote desirable pupil behaviour?
3. What factors are believed to influence pupils' classroom behaviour in a positive/negative way?
4. How could teachers be supported in the effective management of pupil behaviour?

1   2   3   4

A   B   C   D

Data

A. Teachers' questionnaire – perceptions, attitudes, beliefs and behaviours
B. Pupils' group interviews – perceptions, attitudes, influences and behaviours
C. Researcher observations – behaviours, strategies, ethos/culture
D. School policy documents – ethos/culture, strategies

Fig. 10.1 ◆ Matching key research questions to sources of data

Essentially, the presentation and analysis of your data is not something that you should start to consider once you have collected your evidence. It needs to be part of the initial research design and influential on the research approach and methodology, so that by the time that you get to this stage the transfer of the evidence into your report or assignment should be as smooth as possible.

It may prove difficult, but it is important to recognise that not all of the information that you have collected will be needed for your research. Be selective in what data you choose to include within the text of your report or assignment (your full findings can always be placed in an attached appendix). However, it is equally important that you collect a full range of evidence in the first place – it is always much easier to collect the data then not use it, than not collect it and later wish that you had.

Qualitative and quantitative data

Whilst qualitative evidence is most often associated with the interpretive paradigm, and quantitative with the positive/normative, which may suggest that the evidence collected will be of one form or the other, in many cases research evidence will be a combination of both forms. Where a single form of evidence has been gathered, the presentation of it can follow through directly from the guidance suggested by the approach and methodology.

Thomas (2003:1) distinguishes between qualitative 'describing … characteristics of people and events' and quantitative 'measurements and amounts … of the characteristics displayed'. So quantitative evidence will provide an indication of the scale or relative importance of an issue (or problem), whilst qualitative evidence will attempt to offer an interpretation or explanation. Given these differences, combining evidence from these forms can significantly add to the strength and depth of an argument. The statistics can often be used to 'grab' the attention of the reader ('eight out of ten cats said their owner preferred …'), but it is left to the qualitative evidence to make a connection at a deeper level (the picture of the well-fed cat and purring owner) to give 'life' to the numbers. Due thought and consideration should be given as to how these forms can be combined to ensure the greatest impact.

Research reports that make effective use of both quantitative and qualitative data will often lead with the quantitative evidence to provide an immediate point of impact as a 'headline', and then follow it up and enrich the interpretation and analysis through the introduction of the qualitative sources.

Presenting qualitative data

Qualitative data, by its very nature, is more open to ambiguity and requires the identification of emergent key themes for it to be organised and collated and interpreted. Responses are likely to be unique to each individual respondent so the researcher needs to be alive to the potential patterns that might exist and be aware of opportunities for categorisation. While qualitative data can be used very effectively to identify a pattern or trends in relation to a specific phenomenon, it has its limitations with regard to providing explanations for the underlying reasons and the way in which it can give voice to those participating in the research and thus represent their perspective.

Due to the linguistic or visual nature of much of what is construed as qualitative data, the role of the researcher in the selection and interpretation of the evidence is crucial to the success and validity of the research. All potential for bias should have been acknowledged at an earlier stage and the conceptual literature should be used to justify the coding and data organisation.

To a very large extent, where qualitative data has a benefit over quantitative data, at this level, is in the depth and exemplification that it is able to offer. Qualitative data can be collated and aggregated to provide numerical responses, but the real strength is in the way that quoting from respondents is able to offer insight and humanity into the analysis. It is concerned with 'meanings and the way people understand things' (Denscombe, 2003: 267). When presented in narrative, it provide tones and a means of helping the reader to 'connect' with the research that pure numerical data is unable to convey. By using quotations from interviews, observations, diaries or questionnaires; depth and greater meaning can be added to quantitative data, but needs to be employed with care to avoid being perceived as 'anecdotal' so referencing to the respondent(s) is important.

An effective analysis involves:

◆ clear exposition of complex arguments and issues;
◆ identifying causal relationships;

◆ elucidating and explaining;
◆ sustaining a logical argument;
◆ comparing and contrasting;
◆ identifying and challenging assumptions; and
◆ explaining.

When presenting qualitative evidence, the source should be clearly identified in some appropriately coded way that distinguishes between respondents but does not individually identify them. This is to allow different responses from the same respondent to be acknowledged. The identifiers can be very simple, for example,

◆ R_1, R_2 for the different respondents; or
◆ T_1, T_2 for 'teachers' or 'tutors' and S_1, S_2 for students.

The transcripts of the interviews or qualitative elements of questionnaires, observations or documents should be placed in appendices and appropriately referenced to in the text of the study.

Presenting quantitative data

Quantitative data provides your study with impact – '85% of parents (n=38) claimed that …' does suggest that the claim (whatever it might be!) has significant backing and support and is worth taking note of (assuming, of course, that you have followed the guidance in chapter 4 and used an appropriate sample!). (Note that where a percentage is used, it should be accompanied by the population size.)

USE OF TABLES

In most cases, the best place to collate and organise the quantitative data that you have collected is on a spreadsheet. Each column will be used to record the response from a different question and each row a different respondent. Hopefully you will find, if you have constructed your questionnaire or document/observation recording schedule well, that once you have inputted the data, the organisation, sorting and tabulation of the data can be achieved with relative ease.

Table 10.1 ◆

Methods of praise which each group feels pupils will value the most			
Methods of praise	Pupils	Parents	Governors
Verbal	19%	21%	40%
Commendations	8%	21%	10%
Letters home	56%	43%	35%
Certificates	11%	12%	15%
Other	5%	3%	0%
Total responses	205	121	20

As well as for organisational purposes, tables should also be considered for the presentation of data, especially where the data is succinct and well contained with the potential for comparative interpretation:

In Table 10.1 all of the data has been converted to percentages in order to make the comparisons more self evident. Please note that the actual number of respondents for each sub-population has been retained to ensure that the scale of the response is not hidden. It is important to not only provide each of your tables with a title which clearly explains the content, but also with a reference – the one above, Table 10.1, is the first table in the tenth chapter of this book.

USE OF GRAPHICS

The impact of numerical data can often be further enhanced and simplified through the use of tabulated or graphical presentation, however the data does need to be explained and interpreted and contextualised, do not expect the numbers alone to be sufficient. In terms of graphical representations of data, it is important to ensure that the correct format is employed for the data being used. Where mutually exclusive, categoric data sets, such as in the case of responses to a multiple choice question are used, such as:

The meeting with the attention deficit and hyperactivity disorder (ADHD) specialist helped me to understand my child's needs: strongly agree (20) agree (12) disagree (7) strongly disagree (2).

It is possible to use a pie chart which has been appropriately titled (making appropriate use of the question that was posed in the questionnaire) to present this data in

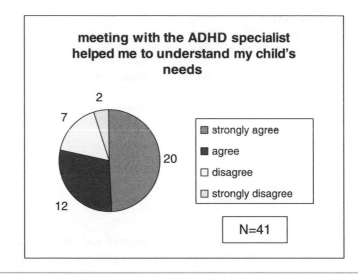

Fig. 10.2 ◆ Pie chart (Source: Burton, 2007:156)

a very clear and explicit way. Pie charts are frequently presented using percentage data, but should also indicate the total number of responses (N = 41) and include a legend which identifies the content of the segments (Fig. 10.2).

Pie charts can either be presented in absolute or percentage format, but should always sum to '100%'. Where there is no obvious 'order' to the data sets (unlike the example), it should be organised so that, starting at '12 o'clock' and going clockwise there should be a progression from largest to smallest segment.

Where the comparison is between mutually inclusive categoric data sets (that is, it is possible to respond positively to more than one category) then a bar chart should be used, as the number of responses is likely to exceed the number of respondents. The categories should be organised in some meaningful way – usually by size or by alphabetical order of the category names. In this example the question posed to students in two Year 10 classes was:

Which languages do you speak?

English ○ *Polish* ○ *German* ○ *Arabic* ○ *Urdu* ○ *Other* ○ ....

Which could easily result in more than one response from each respondent.

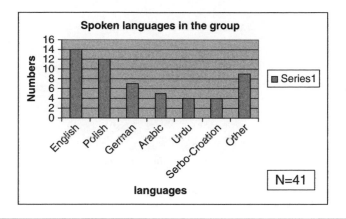

Fig. 10.3 ◆ Bar chart (Source: Burton, 2007: 157)

Whilst the number of respondents is 41, the total number of actual responses is 55. Not only does Fig. 10.3 have a title, the axes are also labelled, as are subsequent graphs. By convention the horizontal (x-axis) is the independent variable (the one that is independently changed) and the vertical (y-axis) is the dependent variable (the one that measured). It is also possible to use bar charts to comparatively present data from different sub-populations (male/female, departments, etc), but the choice of the actual format does need to be chosen sympathetically for the intended audience. Figure 10.4 compares the duties performed by teachers working in different KSs. To complete such a graphic, the data mush have already been aggregated and collated in the form of an average (probably mean) for the groups.

It is possible to represent relationships graphically where both sets of data are presented in numerical form. A table listing reading ages against the chronological age of a group of children may not be particularly easy to assimilate.

In the scatter graph, Fig. 10.5, it is perhaps easier to see that apart from the eldest child in the group who has a reading age of just over 12, there would appear to be no obvious relationship between chronological and reading age, but a statistical analysis might be called for Figure 10.5 also uses a truncated scale on the x-axis which could present an unrealistic view of the relationship.

Line graphs can be used to display trends over time. In Fig. 10.6 the number of days that a school has needed to employ additional teaching staff has been recorded. However, the graph does need to be read with care to distinguish between cover

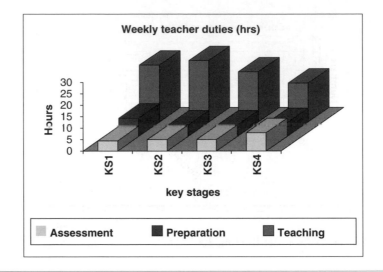

Fig. 10.4 ◆ Stacked bar chart

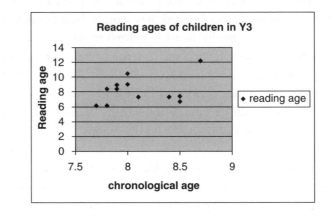

Fig. 10.5 ◆ Scatter graph

for illness (squares), training (triangles), and total (diamonds) and for presentation purposes colour printing would need to be considered.

Figure 10.6 perhaps provides an example of the limits which graphics should not go beyond. There comes a point at which the attempt to provide clarity through a graphical presentation can become counter productive when too much information is included in one place.

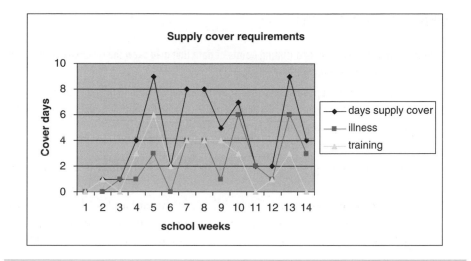

Fig. 10.6 ◆ Line graph

It is important to recognise that a balance is required between the data included within the text and the data presented within an appendix. Too much information presented in the text of a dissertation or report will reduce the quality of the 'flow' of the argument being presented, too little and the reader will be forced to search for meaningful data to support the analysis being made. Where, due to available space or to ensure that the flow of the assignment is maintained, data is placed within an appendix it will need to be appropriately referenced to ensure that the reader is able to find it if necessary (the information placed here should be regarded as incidental rather than core). For example, *all* quantitative responses generated in a questionnaire survey could be placed in the appendix, while only those scores directly relevant to a particular research question will be incorporated in the text.

Use of basic statistical tests

Beyond simple presentation of quantitative data statistical tests can be applied to further confirm the validity and reliability of the findings. Often this takes the form of testing the extent to which the data from different populations (the parents and counsellors of ADHD children, for example) differ in their responses or perceptions. As there is insufficient space here to explain the workings and applications of statistical tests only a brief description of the main tools can be offered.

'Averages' – three to chose from:

◆ *Median* – reduces the impact of outlining points of data that may skew the results (list the data in order of magnitude and identify the mid-point).
◆ *Mode* – highlights the most popular response (but there may be more than one of them!).
◆ *Mean* – incorporates all the data, but can be adversely affected by 'outliers' (data points which are very different from the rest – unusually large or small in comparison).

For example, the reading ages of a second group of Year 3 children (see Table 10.2):

There are three different 'averages'; 7.5 (median), 8.2 (mean) and 8.4 (mode). As the researcher and interpreter of the data, it is your responsibility to justify the choice of the 'average' reading age for the group – which version best represents the abilities of the group as a whole?

DATA SPREAD

◆ *Range* – simply the largest minus the smallest (in Table 10.2 this would be 12.2–6.1 = a range of 6.1 years.
◆ *Standard deviation* – provides an indication of the spread of the data around the mean (in this case 1.9 years).

Table 10.2 ◆ Identifying the median and mode

Reading age	
6.1	
6.1	
6.7	
7.3	
7.3	
7.4	
7.5	median
8.4	
8.4	mode
8.4	
9.2	
11.5	
12.2	

◆ *Inter-quartile range* – identifies the range where 50% of the data will lie and is often linked to the median (in the example the inter-quartile range is 7.3 to 8.4 years).

COMPARING DATA FROM DIFFERENT POPULATIONS

This is a particularly popular use of statistics in educational research. The identification of 'differences' between, well defined groups: male and female; different departments; subjects; courses; age groups. Or, alternately, between a 'sub-group' and 'the rest of the population'; for example, those with a particular ethnicity; educational need; or position within the educational hierarchy. In the literature on research methodology this is linked to the use of 'null hypotheses' (Cohen *et al*, 2007; Walliman, 2005) whereby the test will show that there are no 'statistically significant' differences between the evidence from the two sources. By 'statistically significant' we are talking about the differences in the data from the two sources being caused by something more than random chance. Generally, two levels of significance are tested for. A 0.05 level of significance (or 95% level of confidence) – which means that random chance would only lead to the result 1 time out of 20. The 0.01 level of significance means that it would only have happened by chance 1 in 100, that is, you should be 99% confident that the factor that you had identified has caused the difference.

Chi-squared test – compares the extent to which two populations (for example, male and female) have responded differently to the same questions (for example, attendance at training sessions – if there are twice as many males as females eligible to attend the session, the expectation would be for there to be twice as many males actually attending if gender is *not* a factor).

The formula for the test is written as:

$$\chi^2 = \sum \frac{(o - e)^2}{e}$$

Where:
o = observed result; and
e = expected result.

A Chi-squared test is used to ask the questions:

1. Is there a relationship in the data between the two variables?
2. How strong is the relationship in the data?

3. What is the direction and shape of the relationship in the data?
4. Is the relationship due to some intervening variable(s) in the data?

Example: Is the gender balance in a secondary school 'fair'? With the generalisation that there will be a greater proportion of men in management roles:

– is this generalisation reasonable given the data?

Calculating the 'expected' numbers – how many would you expect to be in each category if there was a precisely proportional split, for example, 21 TAs in total. There are 34 males out of 100 staff (34%), if this same proportion were TAs (34% of 21- the total number of TAs) you would expect to find 7.14 of them.

Chi-squared $= 9.53$ (see Table 10.3) – this means nothing on its own!

You need to find the number of degrees of freedom (df) that you are working within. Here we have five categories of staff (TAs to SMT) and M/F for each – ten cells with data in. Putting a line through one row and one column we are left with four cells – 4df. Using the Chi-squared tables (you should be able to find these tables on the Internet) we can check that the generalisation is only going to be wrong 1 time in 20 (a level of confidence of 0.05) look down the 0.05 column and across the 4df row – the figure that you come to is 9.48773. The calculated figure is larger than this (just!) so that we can say with 95% confidence that our generalisation is borne out by the data – that there is an 'unfair' balance of males in management positions.

The same approach could be used to test whether there is any significance in the assertion that girls (or any other population subgroup) perform better (or worse!)

Table 10.3 ◆ Chi-Squared test calculations

Gender	TAs	Teachers	Subj. Lead	Fac. Head	SMT	Total
Male (obs)	3	17	6	5	3	34
Male (exp)	7.14	16.66	6.12	2.38	1.70	
$(o-e)^2/e$	2.40	0.01	0.00	2.88	0.99	**6.29**
female (obs)	18	32	12	2	2	66
female (exp)	13.86	32.34	11.88	4.62	3.30	
$(o-e)^2/e$	1.24	0.00	0.00	1.49	0.51	**3.24**
Totals	21	49	18	7	5	100
						$x^2 = $**9.53**

than the population as a whole, at GCSE, in maths (or any other subject that you have the data for). In mixed ability teaching groups, do some teachers achieve better results than the rest?

'Spearman's rank' – compares the extent to which two populations rank the same list of criteria differently, or the correlation between the rankings of two separate lists by the same population.

Spearman's rank:

$$\rho = 1 - \frac{6 \sum d_i^2}{n(n^2 - 1)}$$

where:
d_i = the difference between each rank of corresponding values of the two populations; and
n = the number of pairs of values.

Example: Teachers and students rank the key features of a successful lesson; $1 =$ most important, $8 =$ least

The closer to 1, ρ is, the closer the correlation between the rankings of the two groups. The closer it is to zero the less correlation there is and the closer to –1 then the correlation is negative – in the example the teachers and the students would rank the features in the exact opposite order! In table 10.4, ρ=0.095, very close to zero,

Table 10.4 ◆ Spearman's Rank calculations

Features	Teachers	Students	Difference^2	
Enthusiasm	5	1	16	
Well planned	2	5	9	
Good resources	6	6	0	
Effective assessment	4	8	16	$\rho = 0.095238$
Practical activities	7	2	25	
Clear objectives	1	4	9	
Good discipline	3	3	0	
Linked to other work	8	7	1	
		$\sum$d squared	76	

suggesting that there is little correlation between the lists of the teachers and the students.

Table 10.5 compares rankings following performance in maths and PE assessments – can KS3 maths SATs be used to predict KS4 PE performance? There is general agreement, in the 'statistical analysis community', that a correlation co-efficient between zero and 0.3 (positive or negative) is an indication that no relationship exists and a very strong relationship between 0.8 and 1 (positive) or –0.8 and –1 (negative). A co-efficient of 0.3 would, therefore, be regarded as very weak, progressing in strength as it nears 0.8.

Summary

Even with all of these tests for significance, you must remember that the data needs to be interpreted and explained and placed into context. Simply stating that the test shows that the relationship is unlikely to be the result of pure chance is really only a rather minor part of the process – do not become too obsessed by the statistics to the exclusion of the deeper analysis of the evidence.

More is not always better – ensure that the evidence that you do provide is presented clearly and in sufficient detail, but does not overload the audience with too much information. Succinct is good, dense is not.

Table 10.5 ◆ Comparing the Cohart

Students	Maths	PE	Difference	
A	1	1	0	
B	2	5	9	
C	6	6	0	
D	4	8	16	$\rho = 0.380952$
R	7	2	25	
F	5	4	1	
G	3	3	0	
H	8	7	1	
	$\sum$d squared		52	

FURTHER READING

◆ Burton, N., 'The Research Process' in Zwozdiak-Myers, P. (Ed) *Childhood and Youth Studies*, Exeter: Learning Matters (2007)

◆ Cohen, L., Manion, L. and Morrison, K., *Research Methods in Education* (6th Ed) Abingdon: Routledge (2007)

◆ Pell, A. and Fogelman, K., 'Analysing Quantitative Data', in Briggs, A. J. R. and Coleman, M. (Eds) *Research Methods in Educational Leadership and Management* (2nd Ed) London: Sage Publications (2007)

◆ Thomas, R., *Blending Qualitative & Quantitative Research methods in Theses and Dissertations*, California: Corwin Press (2003)

◆ Watling, R. and James, V., 'Analysing Qualitative Data', in Briggs, A. J. R. and Coleman, M. (Eds) *Research Methods in Educational Leadership and Management* (2nd Ed) London: Sage Publications (2007)

11 Analysing – Comparing Evidence

By the end of this chapter you should:

◆ be able to appreciate the connections and differences between presentation and analysis of findings;
◆ be aware of the need to compare data from different sources; and
◆ understand the importance of comparing the research findings with published research and conceptual frameworks.

In the last chapter we considered different ways of selecting and presenting data with the aim of providing a clear overview and in preparation of analysing the information gathered. After having accumulated a wealth of information you will need to develop a system for its storage and efficient retrieval in relation to specific questions or substantive issues. By the end of this chapter you should have developed an understanding of the principles underpinning data analysis and how it forms a bridge between data collection, interpretation and development of theory.

Data storage and retrieval

As a teacher you are most likely to have employed similar procedures in compiling student records, either manually or electronically, which closely mirror those processes involved in the analysis of research data. A systematic approach to the collection and inputting of assessment items is key to ensure efficient storage and retrieval of often highly disparate information. The following excerpt (Example 11.1) by a trainee teacher contributing to an online History Teachers Discussion Forum (HTDF) aptly illustrates this point:

Example 11.1

I use MsExcel. I think it's great. As a student, I don't have a mark book or register at all, so I have it all done on an MsExcel spreadsheet. One for each class with several worksheets on each one. Each worksheet has a register, a seating plan (one coloured depending on behaviour, one not for printing out and leaving on the desk) and a mark 'book'.

Took me a while to set it all up, but I really do see the benefits when I take books in. I have a standard set of colours and notations.

red = not done

orange = unfinished

pink = work not in book

blue = book not seen

The advantage of the blue is that when I do finally see the book, I know how far back I have to go to make sure it's all marked. I also have a column that tells me how many times I haven't seen their books. So anyone thinking that I won't notice if they just keep 'forgetting' to hand their books in, will get caught out. Has quite a few effects:

(1) I can print out a register and have it in the class file which then gets updated once a week on the computer.
(2) I can see who's doing really well, and who's taking the p*** as they've got a student.
(3) I can hold up a printed out worksheet (names hidden) and show them how it works and how easily I can see what they're doing – they don't like that!!
(4) If I'm asking too much of them, that will be clear too as the whole class will have orange 'unfinished' cells.
(5) When I go, I can hand it over to the usual teacher and all the information they need is there for them.

The main negative side to it is that I haven't yet managed to work out (other than the clearly obviously long winded way) how to link in absences with the pink 'not in book' and the red 'not done' (when relating it to homework).

continued

> Overall, I'm really happy with it, and the teachers I've shown have seemed quite impressed. They've even suggested I take it to parents' evening. Not sure it's that good!

The careful construction of research tools (see chapters 6–8 for specific examples) is central to the effective storage and retrieval of data. If the research tool is designed to collect the data in a meaningful and systematic way, as well as making the process more coherent and easy for the respondents, it should also make the collation and analysis processes much more straightforward for you. By using the conceptual framework derived from your reading as the basis for your collection tools, your data should smoothly link back to your literature for ease of analysis.

Types of evidence

Adopting a mixed methodology (quantitative and qualitative data) is an effective strategy of enhancing the validity of research outcomes. Whilst the quantitative data will often provide the immediate 'impact' of your findings ('85% of students ($n=178$) agreed that), it is often the qualitative findings, particularly direct quotations or observations that exemplify and give 'depth' to the point the findings make. This leads us to the point of analysis, which must not be equated with the sorting and listing of information, but describes the transition from presenting information to detecting patterns, identifying trends and establishing meaningful linkages between various categories of data. At this stage, many researchers feel overwhelmed by a deluge of data. In their endeavour to move from the presentation of data to analysis and interpretation they often refer to this stage as 'hitting a brick wall'. In this situation it is helpful to return to the original research question and objectives to see whether they can provide an initial impetus in the identification of key categories which restore some order in the data chaos. As highlighted by Robson (2002) 'overload is a constant danger' and 'the main difficulty lies in their analysis' (2002: 456). Software packages such as NUD*IST and N-VIVO can provide useful tools for the systematic storage and retrieval of data and thus induce the process of analysis in a less painful and more manageable way. Another way which we have found to be highly therapeutic and helpful in releasing creative energies is through drawing of diagrams. By allowing your ideas and associations to roam freely outside an existing structure, new, unexpected categories and linkages are generated, which can be incorporated in the conceptual framework underpinning the story you would like to tell.

Maintaining focus and coherence

It goes without saying that the aim of any research project is to seek answers to questions posed. In most cases, at least initially, it is those questions or research objectives that provide some of the key concepts around which data collection will be constructed. However, it is possible that new and unexpected concepts will emerge, which are entirely relevant to the focus of the research and therefore have to be taken into account in the overall analysis and interpretation of data. The most appropriate response to identifying these unexpected concepts is to complete a further search of the literature to see if these findings are either replicated elsewhere or are consistent with conceptual models that you had not previously considered – either way a revision of your literature review would be the expected outcome.

The organisation of the analysis will tend to be most effective where the initial research questions, posed in the introduction to the study, are employed as the structural device. In this way data from the various sources, both in terms of research populations (and sub-populations) and research tools are combined to address each question in turn. Once the data you have collected have been comparatively analysed, they then need to be brought into analytical contact with both the theoretical models and perspectives, appropriate to the focus of the study, and the outcomes of published research, which will already have been analysed in your review of the literature.

It would be simplistic to assume that the process of relating data to the various research questions/objectives is of a linear nature. Some data sets may only be relevant to one research objective, while others may be used to provide answers to several research questions, and others, yet again, may be entirely irrelevant and therefore need to be discarded, however painful this may be to the researcher. First of all, however, you need to code your data in preparation for analysis.

Coding – breaking down and reassembling of data

Whether in regard to quantitative or qualitative data, coding is generally used as a shorthand to identify the data and allocate them to a system of categories and sub-categories. We generally differentiate between pre-determined codes, which can be borrowed from the literature or existing models and frameworks and open codes, emerging naturally from the data during collection, analysis and interpretation. While the former are more akin to a deductive approach, the latter are used inductively. In this sense coding is not be understood exclusively as a technical activity, but as an organic, interactive process, which also includes the use of literature as highlighted by Strauss and Corbin (1998: 49–52). For they believe that concepts emerging from the data can be compared in terms of their properties and dimensions and that reading of the literature can act as a sensitising device, making the researcher aware of subtle nuances in the data. It can also be used to explore, confirm and clarify concepts used in the categorisation of data. In addition, you will draw on your professional practice knowledge (Eraut, 1984) and personal experience to ensure that the codes and categories used in your analysis of data are valid and meaningful (Fig. 11.1).

For example, by listening to interview recordings prior to, during and after coding, and reading of transcripts and interview responses, line by line, word by word, texts can be analysed in a rigorous and systematic manner. Accordingly, 'data are broken down, conceptualised and put together in new ways', a process within 'one's own and other's assumptions are explored and leading to new discoveries' (Strauss & Corbin, 1990:57;62).

Thus categories for analysis can be derived from a variety of sources, including one's own assumptions, hunches and hypotheses as well as allowing for the emergence

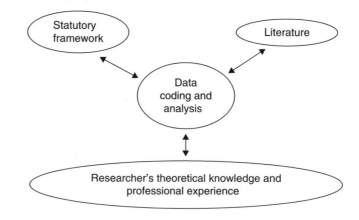

Fig. 11.1 ◆ The dialogical process of data analysis

of new concepts (Tesch, 1990). The following example illustrates the generation of codes and sub-codes.

Example 11.2 – Coding

An evaluative case study of NQTs' experience of induction in the year of the implementation of the statutory induction framework 1999

The study followed a predominantly qualitative approach. Data were collected by means of semi-structured questionnaires and F2F, recorded interviews with newly qualified teachers prior to, during and on completion of induction and half-way through the year with their induction tutors. Initially, the four cornerstones on which the induction framework rested, namely 'support', 'guidance', 'monitoring' of progress and 'assessment' of competence, provided the key codes for analysis. However, as the process of data collection, coding and analysis unfolded it became irrevocably clear that additional codes and sub-codes would be required to capture the entirety of NQTs' experiences and the issues arising from it. Questionnaire responses and interview transcripts were examined systematically, line by line, word by word with the objective of developing an organically growing coding system in relation to the focus of the study. For example, the concept of support manifested itself in various forms and originated from a wide range of sources, as illustrated below.

1 Support

1.1 NQTs' expectations

1.2 Statutory entitlement

1.3 Support provided by

1.3.1 Induction tutor

1.3.2 Head of department

1.3.3 Colleagues

1.3.4 Teaching assistants

1.3.5 Other school staff

1.3.6 Peers

Continued

1.4 Local authority

1.5 Formal, structured programme

1.5.1 Internal

1.5.2 External courses

1 6 Informal support systems

1.7 Examples of support

1.7.1 Collaborative planning, teaching and assessment

1.7.2 Lesson observation and constructive feedback

1.7.3 Observation of good practice

1.7.4 Learning conversations

In addition to the four pre-determined (*a priori*) codes new concepts emerged from the data. In selecting appropriate codes the researcher often referred to her own experience as a NQT, mentor of trainees and PGCE tutor and her professional practice and theoretical knowledge acquired over the years, bringing various perspectives to bear. For example, 'Expectations', 'Challenges', 'Successes', 'Disappointments' and 'Coping strategies' were categories considered relevant and emerging from the data. These codes intersected with the respondents' own 'in-vivo' (live) codes, such as 'Raring to go', 'Finding one's feet' or 'Home and dry', which aptly described the three sequential phases commonly associated with induction: initial enthusiasm, tempered by the realisation that in spite of enormous challenges they were beginning to establish themselves as teachers, and finally, having their qualified teacher status confirmed.

Further, new and unexpected codes were generated from the data and verified by the literature concerned with the induction of NQTs, such as the notion of 'professional values' and 'the need for pastoral care', both of which were absent in the statutory framework.

Example 11.2 demonstrates that data analysis is a complex and intricate process, which involves more than simply sorting information items and proceeds in a non-linear and unpredictable manner. In this sense it is to be perceived as a continuous dialogue that takes place between the data themselves, pre-determined and emergent codes, relevant practical and theoretical perspectives (including government frameworks and the research literature) and, last but not least, the researcher's own professional practice knowledge.

Intricate process of data analysis

As we have already established earlier, data analysis consists of a number of strategies, which involves the filtering, linking and distilling of a diverse body of information. All three processes serve to identify data that are related to the focus of the study and respond to the research questions/objectives. Such data may be of a quantitative and/or qualitative nature and, particularly in practitioner action research, result in new concepts to be incorporated in the overall research design or new questions to be asked for the purpose of follow-up investigations. Whilst the filtering or 'reduction of data' (Gray, 2004:321) through constant comparison with the research objectives and tentative propositions aims to achieve succinct and coherent findings, the method of triangulation is used to enhance the validity of outcomes. This can be achieved by combining different data sources, perspectives, settings, times and methods and looking for convergent messages, thereby strengthening the validity of a claim. As with every investigation the ultimate goal is to tell a story (Wolcott, 1994). However, this involves more than simply listing a collection of data. This is the point where the creative dimension of the research process comes to the fore. In order to discover what lies beneath the surface of data presented (see chapter 10) in various formats (graph, diagram, table, rankings, listings; narrative) we need to engage in critical analysis. By identifying emerging patterns or trends we can explore potential linkages in our endeavour to understand and explain the underlying reasons for certain phenomena. Analysis could thus be conceived as a dialogue that takes place between the description and interpretation of data or a mutually interdependent process (see Fig. 11.1), where analysis informs interpretation and vice versa. As mentioned earlier, the role of literature forms an integral part of this process. This view resonates with Strauss and Corbin who believe that:

> the interplay of reading the literature and doing an analysis of it, then moving out into the field to verify it against the reality can yield an integrated picture and enhance the conceptual richness of the theory' (1990: 55).

Particularly where the emergence of new codes is concerned, reference to the research literature can enhance their validity, while further reading can result in the discovery of new, relevant codes which hitherto have not been included in the analysis. In addition, it is commonly accepted as good practice to involve more than one researcher in the analysis of data, as it can provide further perspectives (triangulation) and an element of consistency with the aim of enhancing the validity of outcomes and trustworthiness of the research.

Enhancing the validity of research outcomes

In traditional research, validity, reliability and generalisability constitute the essential quality criteria, the latter two of which are difficult, if not impossible, to fulfil by qualitative researchers undertaking small-scale investigations within their own practice setting. Whilst quantitative data analysis makes use of statistical procedures that lend themselves to enhancing the validity, reliability and generalisability of research findings in a scientific/positivistic sense, qualitative researchers undertaking small-scale investigations in their own practice setting frequently employ alternative quality criteria. If a sample is representative, 'findings can be legitimately generalised to a wider population', (Bryman, 1988: 35), but, given the idiosyncratic character of practitioner research, claims for generalisability and reliability beyond the research setting are problematic. Similar problems arise with regard to fulfilling the criterion of reliability, which refers to the degree of consistency with which instances are assigned to the same category by different observers or by the same observer on different occasions. (Hammersley, 1992: 67). Unlike in a science laboratory, there will never be any two schools or classrooms where conditions for learning and teaching are identical and where these processes can be replicated. We also need to accept that practitioner research is typically provoked through teachers' identification of a problem/issue, which warrants systematic enquiry to bring about improvement of the situation. Consequently, it has to defend itself against claims of subjectivity. In this respect it is helpful to refer to Bassey (1999), whose notions of 'internal validity', 'trustworthiness' and 'transferability' are deemed more appropriate. Whilst the validity value will be largely determined by the extent to which the findings are directly related to the issues or problems identified at the outset of the action research cycle and how well they respond to the research questions posed, its 'trustworthiness' is reflected in the selection of appropriate methods and how systematically they have been employed.

Do the data answer the question?

The question whether the data generated answer the research question is central to the process of analysis and relies to a large extent on the appropriate selection of data collection tools. Again, parallels between teaching and research spring to mind in that the methods by which information is compiled must generate valid data. The following situation apparent in the assessment of MFLs is worth considering in this respect, as it raises issues with regard to the validity of data, that is, candidates' responses.

Example 11.3 – Issues of validity in current assessment

The current GCSE and AS/A level examinations in MFLs require pupils to demonstrate competence in understanding and producing the foreign language in speaking and writing.

For example, the listening comprehension requires pupils to respond to questions by extracting relevant information from a text presented to them in the foreign language. While some questions are in English requiring answers in English, others are in the foreign language requiring answers in the foreign language.

What can be said about the validity of the candidates responses if:

(a) They do not comprehend the questions in the foreign language, but can understand the text presented to them in the foreign language?

(b) They are unable to produce the answer in the foreign language, but could give the answer in English?

(c) The questions are in English and pupils are required to respond in English?

Note! The objective of the examination is to assess listening skills in foreign language, not reading (exam questions) **and writing skills** (written responses).

Questions:

1. What are the issues raised in this example?
2. In what way can this issue be transferred to practitioner research?

As Example 11.3 demonstrates, the way in which questions are asked can impair the validity of responses, rendering them worthless for analysis. To prevent this from happening; rigorous scrutiny and systematic piloting of collection tools, such as questionnaires, is considered a standard requirement with the aim of ensuring that the final version is free from any potential misunderstandings and ambiguities.

This is of particular importance where participants with weak literacy skills or low proficiency in English are involved.

METHOD OF TRIANGULATION

One effective strategy employed to enhance the validity of research outcomes is that of triangulation. By bringing together data from different sources, by means of different methods and reflecting different perspectives, the validity of findings can be enhanced considerably (Denzin, 1970; Elliott, 1991) and the trustworthiness of the research process can be strengthened. It plays a key role in the collection and analysis of data and can result in rich, dense data generated from a variety of angles. As in teaching, observation is commonly used to gather information on the teaching and learning process, but other tools, such as questionnaires, interviews, focus group discussion, diaries and logs, audio and video recording, artefacts and supportive documentation are equally acceptable.

To help you understand the principle of triangulation and how it can be incorporated in practitioner research, we would like you to consider Scenario 11.1 and 11.2 and invite you to answer the questions provided.

Scenario 11.1

As part of the national strategy to raise achievement in teaching and learning and as a result of Year 10 pupils' underachievement, your school management intends to implement a mentoring programme involving trainee teachers from the HEI with which they are in partnership. The trainee teachers will act as the pupils' mentors with the aim of providing them with academic and personal support via weekly group and one-to-one meetings. You would like to evaluate the effectiveness of this intervention through an action research approach.

Questions:

1. Whose perspectives do you need to represent in your research team?
2. What kind of data do you intend to collect?

Continued

3. What methods/strategies will you employ in the collection of data?
4. Who will be the research participants from whom you will be seeking information?
5. What kind of data sources will you be using for analysis and why?

Please provide reasons for each of your answers.

Scenario 11.2 – Triangulation of data, methods and perspectives

You are an assistant headteacher of a secondary school with responsibility for staff development. Against the backdrop of restructuring the children's workforce you would like to devise a training and staff development framework for the teaching assistants in your school. The research you are going to undertake is to provide you with data that can inform the development of a professional training and development programme.

The key research questions to which you are seeking answers are as follows:

1. What are their perceptions: teaching assistants' roles and responsibilities?
2. What are their professional and personal needs?
3. How well are they integrated into the school community?
4. In what way and to what extent do they enhance the process of teaching and learning?

You have collected the following data:

- Quantitative data via structured questionnaires (multiple choice) investigating the perceptions of TAs, teaching and clerical staff of TAs' roles and responsibilities.
- Qualitative data via in-depth, F2F, unstructured interviews with TAs, exploring their experiences, feelings and opinions with regard to their status within the children's workforce in general and their specific role within the school.
- focus group discussion with teaching staff viz. TAs' roles and responsibilities;
- lesson observation;

Continued

- informal pupil and parent feedback;
- assessment data;
- pupils' exercise books;
- pupil behaviour and attendance records;
- Ofsted reports;
- school policy;
- staffroom culture and staff relationships; and
- national framework for restructuring the workforce.

Questions:

Which data do you consider most relevant in relation to the research focus and the four key questions posed?

How would you triangulate the data to enhance the validity of findings?

External validation

Finally, if we accept that practitioner research is about collaboration and sharing, we need to ensure that our claim to knowledge or improved practice can stand the test of scrutiny by other critical audiences. One way of enhancing the validity of your findings is to invite members from your community of practice (colleagues, advisers, headteachers) as well as relevant outsiders (Steering group, LA staff, higher education tutors, Children's Services) to act as 'critical friends'. By inviting a wider audience in the analysis and interpretation of data, the information can be re-examined and, if necessary, moderated and thus enhance the validity of the enquiry. For example, the coding labels and categories used in the analysis of data should be examined from a range of perspectives, to ensure that the meaning attached to it by the researcher is shared and understood by others involved in the research. To illustrate the diversity of meanings assigned to a single word by different people, Strauss and Corbin use the example of the word 'red'. Whilst some will associate it with 'bulls, lipstick and blood', in others it might evoke images of 'a favourite dress, a rose, a glamorous sports car, or none of the above' (1998:60). Within the context of action research McNiff (1996:108) provides a helpful model, which can be transferred to any research concerned with educational issues in practice settings. It presents five types of validation by a critical audience:

◆ self-validation – evidence in rigorous approach, for example, triangulation, piloting of tools;
◆ peer validation – feedback from practitioners in your field;
◆ up-liner validation – positive evaluation of your research outcomes by those in authority;
◆ client validation – improvement of service; and
◆ academic validation – feedback from tutor/mentor in higher education.

Finally, refer to the wider academic community at large, against whose theoretical and practical perspectives you can test the validity of the patterns, trends and linkages identified in the process of analysing your data in the literature and in search of further evidence in support of your claims. Make full and extensive use of the literature which you explored to establish a conceptual and empirical basis for your study – now compare your analysis of your findings against it. How do your findings compare with the outcomes that the theoretical literature and the published research led you to expect?

FURTHER READING

◆ Bryman, A., *Quantity and Quality in Social Research*, London: Routledge (1988)

◆ Gray, D. E., *Doing Research in the Real World*, London: Sage, Chapter 13 (2004)

◆ Lincoln, Y. S. and Guba, E. G., *Naturalistic Inquiry*, Newbury Park, CA: Sage (1985)

◆ Robson, C., *Real World Research* (2nd Ed) Oxford: Blackwell, Chapter 14 (2002)

◆ Strauss, A. and Corbin, J., *Basics of Qualitative Research*, London: Sage (1998)

12 Conclusions: Identifying Key Findings and Recommendations

By the end of this chapter you should be able to:

◆ appreciate the need to maintain a consistency between the purposes and the outcomes of the research;

◆ understand the importance of using the research outcomes and the conceptual literature to determine a future course of action; and

◆ be aware of the strengths and weaknesses of the research that has been performed.

This text set out to provide an examination of the need to relate research to personal professional development. The overriding aim that underpins this conception is to engage with new ideas and research findings by testing new practices and evaluating curriculum change through enhanced and formalised reflection. To this end we have attempted to assist the practitioner to understand how research can be used to inform and improve practice; the value of embedding and evaluating initiatives; and, an appreciation of the value of the processes of educational research to the school practitioner.

Research projects and project reports should be clear, well-structured pieces of work that 'hold together' well. There are, however, several factors that militate against the researcher achieving such structural integrity in their work:

◆ practitioner research study is often undertaken in a fractured, interrupted manner;

◆ the literature review may be wide-ranging and, therefore, seem diffuse;

◆ the methodology may adopt an integrative stance that employs blended approaches to research;

◆ the data derived from different research tools or different cases may seem problematic to assimilate; and

◆ it can be difficult to integrate the different elements of conceptual statement, review, methodology and analysis.

This chapter will focus on reiterating the ways in which a research topic can be conceptualised, developed and reported in order to ensure a lucid, comprehensible and unambiguous final research outcomes and recommendations, and also differing approaches to structuring research reports, including dissertations and theses, will be explored. Central to this argument will be the concept that researchers should, from the outset of a project, analyse how they intend to develop the overall structure of their investigation. They should develop a simple 'map' of the project that includes overall structure and sub-structure, ideally constructed in discussion with colleagues or supervisor which will pay dividends. The chapter will also seek to connect the outputs of research with school development and improvement through target setting and strategy enhancement.

Writing research reports – the importance of structure

Throughout this text we have recommended a rational approach to research which has emphasised the identification of researchable problems, the creation of clear research questions and associated aims, and the construction of a research methodology designed to address the research topic in the most productive way. This rational process extends to the final outputs of the research project since clear problems and carefully crafted aims can, ideally at least, lead in to a seamless research report. The construction of an appropriate structure for a research project is vital from the outset because it facilitates:

◆ clarity in the research conceptualisation;
◆ simplicity in the research process;
◆ ease in analysis of data; and
◆ structural integrity in the final thesis.

With these points in mind it is useful to reiterate some of the key points made throughout this text. As has been argued in chapters 2 and 3, the researcher should try to define the research issue or overall question, aim or issue as precisely and in such a way that it cannot be subject to unintended ambiguity. Consequent research sub-questions or research aims should be crafted so as to have equal clarity and such questions should be answerable with the resources that are available and through the methods that the researcher intends to adopt. Too many sub-questions may create unforeseen complexity and cause the research to spiral out of control (about four or five is ideal).

Chapters 5 to 7 outlined the best ways to construct research instruments such as questionnaires and interview schedules by emphasising the use of questions that reflect and investigate research issues stated at the outset of the project. Ideally, these research tools should be structured so that each section of the research tool investigates only one of the research aims (except in the case of certain complex questionnaires where analytical techniques require a complex structure of questions). If employing a blended approach, it is often sensible to use the same order for questions in both surveys and interviews in order to facilitate easy analysis of the data. Chapters 10 and 11 explored in detail some of the many ways of presenting and analysing data, one of the most common of which is the use of a 'stem and branch' analysis that reflects research aims, the order of the questions in your survey, and the order of the topics in the research tools if questionnaires or interviews have been employed as part of the methodology.

This approach will assist in the final writing of the research report since all of the elements of this logical approach will feed in to the writer's account of what happened in the process of research. Such reports can be complex and challenging to write because they contain within them a number of ambiguities and contradictions. The writer needs to tell the 'story' of the research in a way which engages readers but the report must be analytical in nature; the study should help to create new understandings and create new knowledge but it should also synthesise previous research findings and theoretical perspectives; and, the researcher needs to show that they have a mastery of theory but they will also wish to show the practical implications of their findings. However, the paramount challenge is often the necessity to provide a sense of 'narrative flow' whilst ensuring structural integrity within the work. This is because the potentially disjointed nature of a dissertation, thesis or report will tend to militate against the creation of essential linkages between sections. Most dissertations, theses and reports in the field of educational research follow the standard structure of:

◆ abstract;
◆ introduction;
◆ literature review;

◆ methodology;
◆ data presentation and analysis of findings;
◆ conclusion;
◆ references; and
◆ appendices.

These sections are included since they provide an opportunity to explore all of the key elements that make up a research study. There are a number of ways to provide an underpinning device that will act as a thread throughout these sections. In essence all such approaches can be distilled into the idea that the fundamental themes that emerge from the research questions should reappear in each section or chapter. Figure 12.1 outlines more detail of the structure of a research report by suggesting which items should appear in each section.

As Fig. 12.1 implies, general convention dictates the overall structure of the report but there is no 'proper' or universally agreed method of creating a sub-structure for these larger sections. However, the most common, and frequently the most success- ful, method of structuring the smaller elements that make up a report is to employ an iterative process that develops the themes derived from the original research questions. Thus, in the ideal report, the Introduction would 'set the scene' by out- lining the macro context such as government reports, legislation or other initiatives, and the micro context of the institution or institutions within which the research is situated. The author is, in essence, making a clear argument for the relevance of the research and some claim for originality may also be made, which can either be through arguing that the area explored is in some way unmapped territory, or that the context within which the research is operating has not been explored fully in relation to the issue, or even that the methodology employed has not been brought to bear on the topic and so may cast new light on the issue. Crucially, it is custom- ary to state and to justify the research questions or issues that form the basis of the research. These questions will embody themes that can then be used to under- pin the rest of the document. So, for instance, if five major themes emerge in the research questions, these same five themes may form the sub-sections of the Liter- ature Review that will be the succeeding section of the report. The Methodology section is, to some extent at least, an aside from the ongoing threads of the study since its function is to explain and to justify the research methods adopted, to make claims for generalisability (if appropriate), and to assure the reader that proper eth- ical procedures have been carried out. Nonetheless, the methodology section will still reflect the thematic elements of the research since the methodology employed,

Introduction:

Should present the topic.
Present the macro and micro issues that make the topic relevant and important.
Make a claim to originality for the research.
Present and justify the overall research questions/issues.
Present and justify the research sub-questions/aims/issues.

Literature review:

Should summarise the key literature, in depth, on the topic that you have chosen.
Address, in detail, the sub-questions or research aims that you have set yourself.
Present a coherent line of argument about the topic under research.

Methodology section:

Should present and justify the methodological approach that you have employed.
Include a clear, straightforward and unambiguous outline of the methods you have employed
    in terms of sample, tools, and methods of analysis.
Address key, standard methodological issues such as validity, reliability and ethical
    considerations.
Address, where appropriate, the issues associated with being an 'insider researcher'
    (especially when undertaking a case study of one's own institution).

Data presentation and analysis:

Should be structured in accordance with one of three main approaches to presenting and
    analysing data. These include:
    According to research questions/issues.
    According to research tools.
    According to cases.

Conclusion:

Should reiterate the overall topic and the reasons for the investigation.
State the key findings.
Present or represent any 'model' or 'models' that may have been developed.
Suggest any further research that might be pursued.
Outline any inadequacies in the research.
Provide a final statement that may indicate the importance and originality of the research and
    its potential 'impact' on practice.

Fig. 12.1 ◆ Structure of a research report

the tools used, the sample constructed, and the location of the research will all be dictated by the issues that the researcher wishes to explore. The overarching themes will re-emerge with greater clarity in the subsequent Data Presentation and Analysis sections where they may be used as devices to report on the research, often in the form of sub-sections. The thematic approach will reach its denouement in the Conclusion since it will be inevitable that the writer will wish to return to the issues stated right at the start of the study in order to summarise what has been discovered, what recommendations for changes to practice can be made, and what further research might be undertaken.

Scholarly skills – referencing

Any formal research report should reveal that the researcher has high levels of skill and understanding in scholarship and scholarly conventions. This will include such matters as using appropriate conventions in terms of Abstracts, Contents Pages, Lists of Figures, the overall structure and presentation of the document and the use of conventional spelling. One of the most important sets of skills to demonstrate is that associated with appropriate referencing of material in the text of the report. Most research reports in the Social Sciences employ the Harvard referencing system as outlined in Fig. 12.2. However, there are a number of other systems of referencing; requirements may vary from institution to institution and researchers are always well advised to check on the particular expectations that may be placed upon them.

Professional reports to non-specialist audiences

The practitioner researcher may wish, or be required, to provide a report to a non-specialist audience such as a school governing body, governors' sub-committee, parents committee, or the like. With such an audience the conventions of structure that underpin the more formal method of report-writing embodied in a dissertation or thesis may be modified to take account of the level of expertise of the professional discourse of the researcher. Inevitably such reports are likely to be much shorter than a thesis or report to a funding agency and may only contain a few hundred words. Detail may be left out in an attempt to convey key findings, references may be excluded altogether and much of the complex reasoning that goes into a methodology section may be deemed inappropriate. Nonetheless, it is important not to

Collecting material for referencing:

For books record:

author's or editor's name (or names);
year the book was published (bracketed);
titlo of the book (italicised);
if it is an edition other than the first;
city the book was published in; and
the name of the publisher.

For journal articles record:

author's name or names;
year in which the journal was published;
title of the article;
title of the journal (italicised);
page number/s of the article in the journal; and
as much other information as you can find about the journal, for example, the volume and
    issue numbers.

For electronic resources; collect the information as above; also record:

date you accessed the source;
electronic address or email;
type of electronic resource (email, discussion forum, website, etc); and
in addition to these details, when you are taking notes, if you copy direct quotations or if you
    put the author's ideas in your own words, write down the page numbers you got the
    information from.

References or Bibliography:

When you use the Harvard System, you are only usually required to produce a reference list –
    all the sources you have referred to in the text. However, you may also want you to produce
    a bibliography where you list *all* sources you have consulted, but not referred to in the text.

How to list references in a reference list:

Book with one author

Brundrett, M. (2000) *Beyond Competence: the challenge for educational management*,
King's Lynn: Peter Francis Publishing

Continued

Fig. 12.2 ◆ The Harvard Referencing System
(University of Exeter, 2007)

Book with two authors

Burton, N. and Brundrett, M. (2005) *Leading the Curriculum in the Primary School*, London: Sage

Book with three or more authors

Brundrett, M., Burton, N. and Smith, R. (Eds) (2002) *Leadership in Education*, London: Sage

Book with an editor

Brundrett, M. and Terrell, I. (Eds) (2003) *Learning to Lead in the Secondary School*, London: Routledge Falmer

Chapter in a book written by someone other than the editor

Silcock, P. and Brundrett, M. (2006) 'Co-constructing learning in primary schools: new perspectives on pedagogy', in R. Webb (Ed) *Changing Teaching and Learning in the Primary School*, Maidenhead: Open University Press

Books with an anonymous or unknown author

The University Encyclopedia (1985) London: Roydon

Journal articles

Brundrett, M., Rhodes, C. and Gkolia, C. (2006) 'Planning for leadership succession: creating a talent pool in primary schools', *Education 3–13, 34,* 3: 259–268

Website

DfEE (2001) *Supporting the Target Setting Process,* London: DfEE accessed at http://www.standards.dfes.gov.uk/ts/pdf/DfES_065_2001.pdf [Online], on 20 August 2007

Fig. 12.2 ◆ Continued

patronise such an audience, and the same essential structure of context, main aims, previous perspective, main approach to the research, and main findings can be used to powerful and persuasive effect. One simple method of conveying central messages swiftly is to provide an *Executive Summary* in the form of a few main bullet points at the start of the report. This approach, often combined with a very clear set of *Conclusions and Recommendations* can be very effective in leading agreement on changes in practice.

Ask yourself

What is the audience for my report? Is this a professional audience or a group of stakeholders who may not have specialist knowledge? Have I targeted my report accordingly?

Is the structure of my report correct?

Have I taken account of the appropriate conventions for report-writing for my audience?

Is the presentation of my report as clear as it can be?

Using research outcomes to inform practice

Burton and Brundrett (2005) draw on the work of Fullan (1993; 1999; 2003) to argue that the increasingly diverse nature of societies, the revolution in communications technologies, and new attitudes to learning, have ensured that complexity and change are an unavoidable part of life in schools. In recent years teachers have become expert at development planning and strategic management can be seen as an attempt to insert a rational model on to the frequently disordered and fluctuating circumstances that schools find themselves in (Morrison, 1998: 13). If such change does not lead to sustained improvement that helps pupils and staff the innovation has not only failed in its targets and goals it has also cause a great deal of distress for no reason. The best models of change integrate these issues of complexity, moral purpose and the need for sustained and embedded improvement by suggesting that organisational change in schools is based on a number of key factors that echo throughout this text and include: engagement of parents and community resources; access to new ideas; professional community; internalising responsibility for change; strategic educational planning (Bryk et al, quoted in Fullan, 1999: 35). Practitioner research can provide a formidable toolkit for analysing the complex social situations that obtain in classrooms in order to influence school strategy and target setting.

As a general working definition can be seen as 'the broad overall direction that an organization wishes to move in' (Fidler, 2002: 9). In this sense strategy can be seen as the *big picture* or the *long term set of goals* for a school. We must also remember that any good strategy 'involves the whole organization in a holistic way' (Fidler, 2002: 9) and so, quite simply, if a strategy is to be effective, then it must encourage the involvement of as many people as possible so that they have a sense of ownership and will want to take the strategy forward rather than fighting against it or ignoring its most salient points. It has been argued that strategy development can be seen as a 'conveyor belt with short-term plans working their way through and then dropping off the end of priorities or translating themselves into the completion of one element of longer-term planning' (Fidler, 2002: 11). Burton and Brundrett (2005) draw on the work of Davies and Davies (2003; 2005: 13) to suggest a four-stage 'ABCD' approach to translating strategy into action as shown in Fig. 12.3 below.

As Brundrett and Terrell (2004) point out, the key point to keep in mind about this process is that it should *not* simply be a bureaucratic exercise. If it is managed well it is a means of ensuring that the actual process of accountability is systematised and ordered – an issue that will be analysed further in the succeeding chapter. Development planning is now well established in schools and subject leaders, as the school's middle managers, have a pivotal role to play in its construction and implementation. The key to its success is the extent to which it provides a clear sense of direction which everyone in the subject and senior management team can follow and understand. The standard structure and organisation for what has become known

Articulate	1	Strategy
Build	2	Images Metaphors Experience
Create	3	Dialogues – conversations Cognitive/mental map Shared understanding
Define	4	Strategic perspective Outcome orientation Formal plans

Fig. 12.3 ◆ ABCD approach of translating strategy into action (Davies and Davies, 2005: 204)

as the planning cycle, involves the following key stages: *audit, vision, construction, implementation and evaluation.* This cyclical process helps to provide practitioners with answers to several important questions, including:

◆ Where are we now? (*audit*)
◆ Where do we want the developing subject/department to be in five years time? (*vision*)
◆ What changes do we need to make? (*construction*)
◆ How shall we manage these changes? (*implementation*)
◆ How shall we know whether our management of change has been successful? (*evaluation*)

This cycle has close associations with the school improvement model that is outlined below and with the action research model outlined in chapter 9. The DfES *Guidance for LEAs on Target-setting at Key Stages 2, 3 and 4 for School Attendance* (page 2) outlines a number of key principles for school performance targets and suggests that school targets should be:

◆ based on the prior attainment and expected progress of individual children in each cohort;
◆ ambitious;
◆ focused on equity as well as excellence; and
◆ owned.

The notion of benchmarked and ambitious targets accords with the thrust of all the policy on targets in recent years but the focus on equity and ownership is an interesting and new emphasis. The desire for equity came about because improvements in pupil attainment had not been spread evenly across all groups of pupils. This marks an acceptance of the notion that has been prevalent in school effectiveness and improvement circles that in-school differences may actually be more significant than between school differences. The concept of ownership reflects much of the recent thrust on schools as learning organisations and may be one further indicator of a national acceptance of recent theories of distributed leadership and management. It is notable that this should be: 'A whole-school approach to target-setting, which involves not just headteachers and leadership teams, but also class teachers and, where appropriate TAs, will ensure that the process is fully informed and rigorous' (page 3). This inclusion of TAs no doubt indicates the complex and challenging focus on workforce remodelling. Since such activities operate at the complex level of the individual classroom it is only through the sponsorship of the systematic exploration of personal practice that schools can hope to deliver on such laudable aims.

The DfEE (2001) *Supporting the Target Setting Process* suggests that schools should adopt a policy of target setting within a cycle of school self-improvement as part of a systematic approach to raising standards of pupil achievement. It is suggested that in most schools, KSs and expected National Curriculum levels are suitable timescales and measures for use in setting such targets – although these timelines may need to be amended for pupils with special needs. 'Targeting for improvement in this way serves as a focus for action planning, and as a basis for defining success criteria when monitoring and evaluating the effectiveness of the actions that the school has implemented' (page 6). The document suggests a five-stage cycle of self-improvement as represented in Fig. 12.4.

Step 1 How well are we doing?

Teachers assess what pupils have achieved in relation to the curriculum taught, where possible and appropriate, benchmarked against other, similar groups of pupils from within the school, either in the past or present. In most schools, National Curriculum level descriptions set the standards to use in English, mathematics and science, and pupils' performances at the end of a KS are appropriate as measures of the school's overall. Schools may also consider some pupils' achievements in terms of their acquisition of independence skills based on judgements about the frequency of teacher interventions necessary during their learning. The challenge for schools is to identify the kinds of performance information that are available to show what their pupils are achieving and about which such questions can be asked. For those schools it may be important to first take stock of how pupils' performance is assessed throughout the school and to consider how the school's assessment criteria, data collection systems, and record keeping (page 7).

Step 2 How do we compare with similar schools?

Teachers consider how well the school is doing, shown by its pupils' achievements, in the wider context of the performances achieved by similar pupils in other schools. Local and national benchmark information should enable like for like comparisons to be made. The performance criteria used in the national benchmark information is the proportion of pupils achieving the expected National Curriculum level, or better, at the end of KSs 1, 2 and 3, and GCSE grades and GCSE/GNVQ points scores at the end of KS 4. This information may stimulate key questions such as: *'how do those better performing schools achieve what*

Continued

Fig. 12.4 ◆ Five steps in the cycle of school improvement
  (Burton and Brundrett, 2005.)

they do?' and *'what can we learn from those schools to raise the standards of achievement of our own pupils?'* (page 9).

Step 3 What more should we aim to achieve this year?

Targets are set to drive school improvement and provide impetus and challenge complacency. Statutory targets apply to all schools but all schools can set additional targets that reflect relevant priorities. These additional targets can also be published alongside statutory targets in the school's annual governors' report to parents (page 12). To be effective, targets for school improvement, statutory or otherwise, need to be **SMART** targets. This means they should be: **S**pecific, **M**easurable, **A**chievable and **R**ealistic, and set against an appropriate **T**imescale. SMART targets will be measurable, and reflect the criteria used for measuring pupil performance. Teachers make judgements about translating practice into gains in pupils' performances in the future by deciding what more pupils will achieve when more successful teaching practices are implemented, over and above what they would be expected to achieve given current teaching practice. Those outcomes are the school's measurable targets (page 13).

Steps 4 & 5 Taking action

Having analysed the school's performance and set targets for school improvement, schools move from reviewing performance to taking action. Thus the shared and agreed picture of the school's performance and clear targets for improvement turn to action planning. Action plans identify what is needed to achieve the targets, including the important changes that need implementing and how the action plan is to be supported with resources and staff development. Taking action may involve 'process targets', such as improving accommodation or integration opportunities which will contribute to the school's ability to meet its performance targets. It is important to put in place effective strategies to monitor and evaluate gains in pupils' performance as the new teaching practices take effect (page 17).

Fig. 12.4 ◆ Continued

Such target setting is increasingly informed by the use of national data that is progressively becoming accessible to senior managers and teachers. Practitioner research can serve to unpack the issues that may be identified in comparative data, may serve to challenge the presumed causations of perceived school inadequacies, may identify unforeseen issues, and may suggest means to remediate and overcome inadequacies in a wide range of areas such as approaches to learning and teaching, leadership and management structures, or relationships with the community of stakeholders. All of this will only be achieved if the research that is carried out meets a perceived need, is rigorous in approach, and persuasive in reporting.

Ask yourself

Who are the key stakeholders that my research needs to be communicated to?

Have I met the needs of that audience?

What are the target setting and strategic implications of my work?

How can my research findings be fed into the development cycle of my organisation?

Conclusions

The influential work of academic commentators such as Hopkins (1985) has established the powerful role of practitioner research in school effectiveness and improvement. It can be argued that government agencies could do more to sponsor research activity in schools and may tend to have a narrow and somewhat positivist view of research but there is strong evidence that there is an increasing willingness to support the notion of teaching as an evidence-based profession (Burton and Bartlett, 2005: 182). Throughout this text we have argued that by establishing the links between the teaching and research processes, practitioners will be able to more effectively develop the skills and attributes that underpin the highest quality teaching and learning.

Many professions have become increasingly technical and in recent decades there are many who fear a loss of autonomy amongst practitioners who are progressively more subject to national directives and strategies designed to enhance effectiveness. Practitioner research, if carried out with vigour, confidence, proficiency and skill can enable the professional to re-capture ownership of vital elements of school life. Such research provides a set of analytical tools that can inform, and indeed transform, learning and teaching, and enhance school effectiveness so that outcomes are improved and teachers feel more confident about their continued centrality and creativity in the learning process.

FURTHER READING

◆ Brundrett, M. and Burton, N., *Leading the Curriculum in the Primary School*, London: Sage (2005)

◆ Brundrett, M. and Terrell, I. (Eds) *Learning to Lead in the Secondary School: Becoming an Effective Head of Department*, London: RoutledgeFalmer (2004)

◆ Davies, B. and Davies, B., 'Strategic leadership', in Davies, B. (Ed) *The Essentials of School Leadership*, London: Paul Chapman Publishing: 10–30 (2005)

◆ Fidler, B., *Strategic Management for School Development: Leading Your School's Improvement Strategy*, London: British Educational Leadership, Management and Administration Society/ Paul Chapman Publishing (2002)

◆ Fullan, M., *Change Forces: Probing the Depths of Educational Reform*, London: Falmer Press (1993)

Bibliography

Chapter 1

◆ Cohen, L., Manion, L. & Morrison, K. (2007) *Research Methods in Education* (6th edn) Abingdon: Routledge

◆ GTC (2007) *Teacher Learning Academy: the TLA framework* accessed at http://www.gtce.org.uk/tla/tla_fwk/stage_booklets/stage3/ on 21/5/07

◆ Hattie, J. & Marsh, H.W. (1996) 'The Relationship between Teaching and Research: A Meta-Analysis', *Review of Educational Research*, 66(4), pp 507–542

◆ HEA (2007) *Development and Recognition* accessed at http://www.heacademy.ac.uk/34.htm on 30/5/07

◆ Smyth, J. (1989) 'Developing and sustaining critical reflection in teacher education', *Journal of Teacher Education*, 40(2), pp 2–9

◆ Souter, N. (2007) 'Applying for PGCE, sorry, PGDE, in Scotland?', *Science Teacher Education*, 48 pp 6–8

◆ SVUK (2007) *Interim Endorsement of new Initial Teacher/Tutor/Trainer Training Qualifications for the Lifelong Learning Sector in England* accessed at http://www.lifelonglearninguk.org/svuk/interim_endorsement_tt_quals.html on 30/5/07

◆ Taber, K. (2007) *Classroom-based Research and Evidence-based Practice*, London: Sage Publications

◆ TDA (2007) *Postgraduate Professional Development* accessed at http://www.tda.gov.uk/partners/ppd.aspx on 21/5/07

Chapter 2

◆ Cohen, L., Manion, L. & Morrison, K. (2007) *Research Methods in Education* (6th edn) Abingdon: Routledge

◆ Denscombe, M. (2003) *The Good Research Guide* (2nd edn) Maidenhead: Open University Press

◆ DfES (2005) *Every Child Matters: change for children* accessed at http://www.everychildmatters.gov.uk/aims/ on 21/6/07

◆ DfES (2007) *Publications* accessed at http://www.dfes.gov.uk/publications/ on 18/6/07

◆ Fox, M., Martin, P. & Green, G. (2007) *Doing Practitioner Research*, London: Sage Publications

◆ GTC (2007) *About the GTC* accessed at www.gtce.org.uk/aboutthegtc/ on 21/6/07

◆ Hitchcock, G. & Hughes, D. (1995) *Research and the Teacher* (2nd edn) London: Routledge

◆ HMIe (2007) *Untitled Home Page* accessed at http://www.hmie.gov.uk/ on 21/6/07

◆ NC (1999) *National Curriculum Online* accessed at http://www.nc.uk.net/webdav/harmonise?Page/@id=6016 on 21/6/07

◆ NCSL (2007a) *Publications* accessed at http://www.ncsl.org.uk/publications/index.cfm on 21/6/07

◆ NCSL (2007b) *Programmes* accessed at http://www.ncsl.org.uk/programmes/index.cfm on 21/6/07

◆ Niace (2007) *An Individual Learning Plan* accessed at http://www.niace.org.uk/projects/learningfromexperience/EBS/Good-Practice/ILP.htm on 21/6/07

◆ Ofsted (2007) *Self-evaluation and school performance statistics* accessed at http://www.ofsted.gov.uk/schools/dataandinformationsystems.cfm on 21/6/07

◆ QCA (2007) *Qualifications and Curriculum Authority* accessed at http://www.qca.org.uk/ on 21/6/07

◆ Standards (2007) *Schemes of Work Welcome* accessed at http://www.standards.dfes.gov.uk/schemes3/ on 21/6/07

◆ Taber, K. (2007) *Classroom-based Research and Evidence-based Practice*, London: Sage Publications

◆ TDA (2007) *Training and Development Agency for schools* accessed at http://www.tda.gov.uk/ on 21/6/07

◆ Teachernet (2007) *Online Publications for School: what you need, when you need it* accessed at http://publications.teachernet.gov.uk/ on 18/6/07

◆ Walliman, N. (2005) *Your Research Project*, London: Sage Publications

Chapter 3

◆ Birley, G. & Moreland, N. (1998) *A Practical Guide to Academic Research*, London: Kogan Page.

◆ EPPI-Centre 2007 (2007a) *Reviews of research evidence are not necessarily rigorous or explicit in their methods of review* accessed at http://eppi.ioe.ac.uk/cms/Default.aspx?tabid=67 on 21/8/07

◆ EPPI-Centre 2007 (2007b) *Why is it important to be systematic?* accessed at http://eppi.ioe.ac.uk/cms/Default.aspx?tabid=69 on 21/8/07

◆ EPPI-Centre 2007 (2007c) *Different types of review* accessed at http://eppi.ioe.ac.uk/cms/Default.aspx?tabid=1915 on 21/8/07

◆ EPPI-Centre 2007 (2007d) *Administrative systems* accessed at http://eppi.ioe.ac.uk/cms/Default.aspx?tabid=1918 on 21/8/07

◆ EPPI-Centre 2007 (2007e) *Synthesis* accessed at http://eppi.ioe.ac.uk/cms/Default.aspx?tabid=178 on 21/8/07

◆ Taylor, D. & Proctor, M. (2007) *The Literature Review: A Few Tips on Conducting It*, University of Toronto accessed at http://www.utoronto.ca/writing/litrev.html on 21/8/07

◆ Thody, A. (2006) *Writing and Presenting Research*, London: Sage.

◆ University of Melbourne (2007a) *Conducting a Literature Review*: accessed at http://www.lib.unimelb.edu.au/postgrad/litreview/gettingstarted.html on 21/8/07

◆ University of Melbourne (2007b) *Conducting a Literature Review: Tips on Critical Reading* accessed at http://www.lib.unimelb.edu.au/postgrad/litreview/criticalreading.html on 21/8/07

Chapter 4

◆ Anderson, P. & Morrow, V. (2004) *Ethics, Social Research and Consulting With Children and Young People*, Barkingside: Barbardos

◆ British Educational Research Association (BERA)

◆ British Education Research Association (BERA) (2004) *Revised Ethical Guidelines for Educational Research*, Southwell: BERA

◆ Coastley, C. & Gibbs, P. (2006) 'Researching Others: Care as an Ethics for Practitioner Researchers', *Studies in Higher Education*, 31 (1), pp 89–98

◆ Cohen, L., Manion, L. & Morrison, K. (2007) *Research Methods in Education* (6th edn) Abingdon: Routledge

◆ Fine, G. A. & Sandstrom, K. L. (1988) *Knowing Children: Participant Observation With Minors.* California: Sage

◆ Gray, D. E. (2004) *Doing research in the real world*, London: Sage

◆ Groundwater-Smith, S. & Mockler, N. (2007) 'Ethics in Practitioner Research: An Issue of Quality', *Research Papers in Education*, 22 (2), pp 199–211

◆ Hill, M. (2005) 'Ethical considerations in researching children's experiences', in S. Greene & D. Hogan (Eds.) *Researching children's experiences: approaches and methods*, London: Sage, pp 61–86

◆ Kemmis, S. & McTaggart, R. (2000) 'Participatory Action Research', in N. K. Denzin & Y. S. Lincoln (Eds.) *Handbook of Qualitative Research* (2nd edn) London: Sage

◆ Lindsay, G. (2000) 'Researching children's perspectives: ethical issues', in A. Lewis & G. Lindsay (Eds.) *Researching Children's Perspectives*, Buckingham: Open University, pp 3–20

◆ Masson, J. (2000) 'Researching children's perspectives: Legal issues', in A. Lewis & G. Lindsay (Eds.) *Researching Children's Perspectives*, Buckingham: Open University Press, pp 34–45

◆ Measor, L. & Woods, P. (1984) 'Breakthroughs and blockages in ethnographic research: contrasting experiences during the changing schools project', in G. Walford (Ed) (1991) *Doing Educational Research*, London: Routledge, pp 59–81

◆ Robson, C. (2002) *Real world research* (2nd edn) Oxford: Blackwell

◆ Schön, D. (1983) *The reflective practitioner*, New York: Basic Books

◆ Sieber, J. E. (1992) *Planning ethically responsible research*, Newbury Park, CA: Sage

◆ Stanley, B. & Sieber, J. E. (Eds.) (1992) *Social Research on Children and Adolescents: Ethical Issues*, London: Sage

◆ Stringer, E. T. (1999) *Action Research* (2nd edn) Thousand Oaks, CA: Sage

◆ United Nations (1989*) Convention on the rights of the child*, Geneva: UN

◆ Walford, G. (1987) *Doing Sociology of Education*, Lewes: Falmer Press

Chapter 5

◆ Bell, J. (2005) *Doing your Research Project*, Buckingham: Open University Press

◆ Bogdan, R. & Biklen, S. (1982) 'Qualitative Research for Education', in J. Wellington, (2000) *Educational Research: Contemporary Issues and Practical Research*, London: Continuum

◆ Cohen, L., Manion, L. & Morrison, K. (2007) *Research Methods in Education* (6th edn) Abingdon: Routledge

◆ Denscombe, M. (2003) *The Good Research Guide* (2nd edn) Maidenhead: Open University Press

◆ Glaser, B. & Strauss, A. (1967) *The Discovery of Grounded Theory*, Chicago: Aldine

◆ Hayes, N. (2000) *Doing Psychological Research: Gathering and Analysing Data*, Buckingham: Open University Press

◆ Kvale, S. (1996) *Interviews*, London: Sage

◆ Locke, K. (2001) *Grounded Theory in Management Research*, London: Sage Publications

◆ Mertens, D. M. & McLaughlin, J. A. (2004) *Research and Evaluation Methods in Special Education*, Corwin: Thousands Oaks

◆ Taber, K. (2007) *Classroom-based Research and Evidence-based Practice*, London: Sage Publications

◆ Walliman, N. (2005) *Your Research Project*, London: Sage Publications

Chapter 6

◆ Bell, J. (2005) *Doing Your Research Project* (4th edn) Buckingham: Open University Press

◆ Cohen, L., Manion, L. & Morrison, K. (2007) *Research Methods in Education* (6th edn) Abingdon: Routledge

◆ Denscombe, M. (2003) *The Good Research Guide* (2nd edn) Maidenhead: Open University Press

◆ Kvale, S. (1996) *Interviews*, London: Sage

◆ Morrison, K. (1993) *Planning and Accomplishing School-centred Evaluation*, Dereham: Peter Francis Publishers

◆ Tuckman, B. (1972) *Conduction Educational Research*, New York: Harcourt Brace Jovanovich

◆ Verma, G. & Mallick, K. (1999) *Researching Education: Perspectives and Techniques*, London: Falmer

Chapter 7

◆ Bryman, A. (2004) *Social Research Methods* (2nd edn) Oxford: Oxford University Press

◆ Bryman, A. & Cramer, D. (1997) *Quantitative Data Analysis*, London: Routledge

◆ Clegg, F. (1994) *Simple Statistics: A Course Book for the Social Sciences*, Cambridge: Cambridge University Press

◆ Cohen, L. & Holliday, M. (1996) *Practical Statistics for Students*, London: Paul Chapman Publishing

◆ Cohen, L., Manion, L. & Morrison, K. (2000) *Research Methods in Education* (5th edn) London: RoutledgeFalmer

◆ Hammersley, M. (Ed) (1993) *Social Research: Philosophy, Politics and Practice*, London: Open University Press

◆ Miles, M. B. & Huberman, A. M. (1994) *Qualitative Data Analysis (2nd edn)* Thousand Oaks, CA: Sage

◆ Robson, C. (1993) *Real World Research* (2nd edn) Oxford: Blackwell

◆ Silverman, D. (2004) *Qualitative Research: Theory, Method and Practice*, London: Sage

◆ Solomon, R. & Winch, C. (1994) *Calculating and Computing for the Social Science and Arts Students*, Buckingham: Open University Press

◆ Thody, A. (2006) *Writing and Presenting Research*, London: Sage

◆ Wragg, E. D. (1999) *An Introduction to Classroom Observation*, London: Routledge

Chapter 8

◆ Cohen, L., Manion, L. & Morrison, K. (2007) *Research Methods in Education* (6th edn) Abingdon: Routledge

◆ Denscombe, M. (2003) *The Good Research Guide* (2nd edn) Maidenhead: Open University Press

◆ Duffy, B. (2005) 'The Analysis of Documentary Evidence' in J. Bell, *Doing your Research Project*, Buckingham: Open University Press

◆ Glaser, B. & Strauss, A. (1967) *The Discovery of Grounded Theory*, Chicago: Aldine

◆ Hayes, N. (2000) *Doing Psychological Research: Gathering and Analysing Data*, Buckingham: Open University Press

◆ Locke, K. (2001) *Grounded Theory in Management Research*, London: Sage

◆ Robson, C. (2002) *Real World Research* (2nd edn) Oxford: Blackwell

◆ Taber, K. (2007) *Classroom-based Research and Evidence-based Practice*, London: Sage Publications

◆ Walliman, N. (2005) *Your Research Project*, London: Sage Publications

Chapter 9

◆ Beresford, P. (1999) 'Making participation possible: Movements of disabled people and psychiatric system survivors' in T. Jordan & A. Lent (Eds.) *Storming the Millenium: The New Politics of Change*, London: Lawrence & Wishart, pp 34–50

◆ Bryman, A. (1988) *Quantity and Quality in Social Research*, London: Routledge

◆ Burton, D. M. & Bartlett, S. (2005) *Practitioner Research for Teachers*, London: Sage

◆ Campbell, A., McNamara, O. & Gilroy, P. (2004) *Practitioner Research and Professional Development in Education*, London: Sage

◆ Capobianco, B. M. & Feldman, A. (2006) 'Promoting quality for teacher action research: lessons learned from science teachers' action research', *Educational Action Research*, 14 (4), pp 497–512

◆ Carr, W. & Kemmis, S. (1986) *Becoming Critical: Education, Knowledge and Action Research*, Lewes: Falmer Press

◆ Coghlan, D. & Brannick, T. (2001) *Doing Action Research in Your Own Organisation*, London: Sage

◆ Cook, T. (1998) 'The importance of mess in action research', *Educational Action Research Journal*, 6 (1), pp 93–109

◆ Creplet, F., Dupouet, O. & Vaast, E. (2003) 'Episteme or practice? Differentiated communitarian structures in a biology laboratory' in M. Huysman, E. Wenger & V. Wulf (Eds.) *Communities and Technologies*, Dordrecht: Kluwer Academic Publishers, pp 43–63

◆ Dadds, M. (1995) *Passionate Inquiry and School Development*, London: Falmer

◆ Dadds, M. & Hart, S. (2001) *Doing Practitioner Research Differently*, London: Routledge

◆ Deem, R. & Brehony, K. J. (1994) *'Why didn't you use a survey so you could generalise your findings? Methodological issues in multi-site case studies of school'*, Governing Bodies after the 1968 Education reform Act [pp 154–169] in D. Halpin & B. Troyna (Eds.) *Researching Education Policy*, London: Falmer

◆ Denzin, N. K. (1970) *The Research in Sociology*, London: Butterworth

◆ Dickens, L. & Watkins, K. (1999) 'Action research: Rethinking Lewin', *Management Learning*, 30(2), pp 127–140

◆ Elliott, J. (1991) *Action Research for Educational Change*, Buckingham: Open University Press

◆ Eraut, M. (1994) *Developing Professional Practice*, London: Routledge Falmer

◆ Gray, D. E. (2004) *Doing Research in the Real World*, London: Sage

◆ Hammersley, M. (1992) *What's Wrong With Ethnography?* London: Routledge

◆ Kemmis, S. (1980) 'Action research in retrospect and prospect' mimeo presented at the Annual General Meeting of the Australian Association for Research in Education, Sydney, November

◆ Kemmis, S. et al (1981) *The Action Research Planner*, Victoria, Australia: Deakin University

◆ Kemmis, S. & McTaggart, R. (Eds.) (1992) *The Action Research Planner* (3rd edn) Victoria: Deakin University Press

◆ Lave, J. & Wenger, E. (1991) *Situated Learning: legitimate peripheral participation*, Cambridge: Cambridge University Press

◆ Lewin, K. (1946) 'Action research and minority problems', *Journal of Social Issues*, 2, pp 34–46

◆ Lewin, K. (1952) 'Group decision and social change', in G. W. Sweanson, T. M. Newcomb & E. L. Hartley (Eds.) *Readings in Social Psychology* (New York, Henry Holt & Co) Reprinted in S. Kemmis & R. McTaggart (1988) *The Action Research Reader* (3rd edn) Geelong: Deakin University Press, pp 47–56

◆ Lomax, P. (1990) 'An action research approach to developing staff in schools' in P. Lomax (Ed) *Managing Staff Development in Schools*, Clevedon: Mulit-Lingual Matters, pp 2–7

◆ McKernan, J. (1991) *Curriculum Action Research*, London: Kogan Page

◆ McNiff, J., Lomaz, P. & Whitehead, J. (1996) *You and Your Action Research Project*, London: Routledge

◆ Schön, D. (1983) *The Reflective Practitioner*, New York: Basic Books

◆ Sieber, J. (1993) 'The ethics and politics of sensitive research', in C. Renzetti, C. Lee & R. Lee (Eds.) *Researching Sensitive Topics*, London: Sage

◆ Somekh, B. (1993) 'Quality in educational research: the contribution of classroom teachers' in: J. Edge & K. Richards (Eds.) *Teachers Develop Teachers' Research: papers on classroom research and teacher development*, Oxford: Heinemann

◆ Stenhouse, L. (1975) *An Introduction to Curriculum Research and Development*, London: Heinemann

◆ Troyna, B. (1995: 403) 'Beyond reasonable doubt? Researching 'race' in educational settings, *Oxford Review of Education*, 21 (4), pp 155–165

◆ Waterson, J. (2000) 'Balancing Research and Action: reflections on an action research project in a social services department', *Social Policy Administration*, 34(4), pp 494–508

◆ Wenger, E. (1998) *Communities of Practice: learning, meaning and identity*, Cambridge, UK: Cambridge University Press

◆ Winter, R. (1998) 'Finding a voice, thinking with others: A conception of action research', *Educational Action Research*, 6, pp 53–68

◆ Winter, R. & Munn-Giddings, C. (2001) *A Handbook for Action Research in Health and Social Care*, London: Routledge

◆ Zuber-Skerritt, O. (Ed) (1996) *New Directions in Action Research*, London: Falmer

Chapter 10

◆ Burton, N. (2007) 'The Research Process' in Zwozdiak-Myers (Ed) *Childhood and Youth Studies*, Exeter: Learning Matters

◆ Cohen, L., Manion, L. & Morrison, K. (2007) *Research Methods in Education* (6th edn) Abingdon: Routledge

◆ Denscombe, M. (2003) *The Good Research Guide* (2nd edn) Maidenhead: Open University Press

◆ Thomas, R. (2003) *Blending Qualitative & Quantitative Research methods in Theses and Dissertations*, California: Corwin Press

◆ Walliman, N. (2005) *Your Research Project*, London: Sage Publications

Chapter 11

◆ Bassey, M. (1999) *Case Study research in Educational Settings*, Buckingham: Open University Press

◆ Bryman, A. (1988) *Quantity and Quality in Social Research*, London: Routledge

◆ Denzin, N. K. (1970) *The Research in Sociology*, London: Butterworth

◆ Elliott, J. (1991) *Action Research for Educational Change*, Buckingham: Open University Press

◆ Eraut, M. (1994) *Developing Professional Practice*, London: Routledge Falmer

◆ Gray, D. E. (2004) *Doing Research in the Real World*, London: Sage

◆ Hammersley, M. (1992) *What's Wrong With Ethnography?*, London: Routledge

◆ History Teachers Discussion Forum (HTDF) (2004) www.schoolhistory.co.uk/forum/index.php?showtopic=3105 [accessed 3rd August 2007]

◆ Lincoln, Y. S. & Guba, E. G. (1985) *Naturalistic Inquiry*, Newbury Park, CA: Sage

◆ McNiff, J., Lomaz, P. & Whitehead, J. (1996) *You and Your Action Research Project*, London: Routledge

◆ Robson, C. (2002) *Real World Research* (2nd edn) Oxford: Blackwell

◆ Strauss, A. & Corbin, J. (1990) *Basics of Qualitative Research, Grounded Theory Procedures and Techniques*, London: Sage

◆ Strauss, A. & Corbin, J. (1998) *Basics of Qualitative Research*, London: Sage

◆ Tesch, R. (1990) *Qualitative Research. Analysis Types and Software Tools*, New York, NY: Falmer Press

◆ Wolcott, H. F. (1994) *Transforming Qualitative Data: Description, Analysis and Interpretation*, Thousand Oaks, CA: Sage

Chapter 12

◆ Brundrett, M. & Burton, N. (2005) *Leading the Curriculum in the Primary School*, London: Sage

◆ Brundrett, M. & Terrell, I. (Eds.) (2004) *Learning to Lead in the Secondary School: Becoming an Effective Head of Department*, London: RoutledgeFalmer

◆ Davies, B. & Davies, B. (2005) 'Strategic leadership', in B. Davies, (Ed) *The Essentials of School Leadership*, London: Paul Chapman Publishing, pp 10–30.

◆ Davies, B. & Ellison, L. (2003) *The New Strategic Direction and Development of the School* (2nd edn) London: RoutledgeFalmer

◆ Fidler, B. (2002) *Strategic Management for School Development: Leading Your School's Improvement Strategy*, London: British Educational Leadership, Management and Administration Society/Paul Chapman Publishing

◆ Fullan, M. (1993) *Change Forces: Probing the Depths of Educational Reform*, London: Falmer Press

◆ Fullan, M. (1999) *Change Forces: The Sequel*, London: Falmer Press

◆ Fullan, M. (2001) *The New Meaning of Educational Change*, London: RoutledgeFalmer

◆ Fullan, M. (2003) *Change Forces with a Vengeance*, London: RoutledgeFalmer.

◆ Morrison, K. (1998) *Management Theories for Educational Change*, London: Paul Chapman

◆ University of Exeter (2007) *Referencing – The Harvard System*, University of Exeter, Department of Lifelong Learning: Study Skills Series, accessed at http://www.education.ex.ac.uk/dll/studyskills/harvard_referencing.htm (Online) 20 August 2007

Index

ABCD approach 183
absenteeism example 129, 130, 131
academic validation 173
access
 gaining 48–9, 72–3
 to documents 116–17
accountability
 regimes of 95, 110
 systematisation 183
action plans 186
action research 66, 124–39
 caveats 138–9
 as constructivist approach to
  knowledge creation 136–8
 cycles 132–3
 definition 127–8
 democratic dimension 127
 ethical considerations 136
 formulating research question 130–2
 identifying general idea 128–9
 nature 125–6
 outcomes 128
 participatory (PAR) 128
 planning project 135–6
 process 132–5
 reflective practice and 125–6
 reporting 138
 starting points 129
 stating hypothesis 131–2
 teaching and 135–6
aggregation 106
AIM (Author's Intended Message) 30
appendix, data in 153
approaches to research 64–8
assessment
 for learning (AfL) 7, 9, 125
 of learning 7, 125
attendance rates 18
attendance records 114
audio recording 84
audit 184
averages 154

balance of power 54–6
bar charts 150–1, 152
base-lines 11, 112
benchmarking 185
BERA 48, 51
bibliography, in research report 180
blogs 86
British Educational Research
  Association (BERA) 48, 51

case studies 66–7, 80
 surveys and 78, 80

categories for analysis 117
change, measuring 106
Chi-squared test 155–7
child obesity example 137
client validation 173
cluster analysis 106
coaching framework example
    134–5
coding 163–6
community of practice 137
competence 57
complexity 182
  reducing 106
concept maps 113
conceptual framework
  data collection tools and 162
  development, literature review
      in 38–40
conceptual synthesis 34–5
confidence levels 155
constant sum 90, 92–3
construction 184
content analysis 119, 120, 122
continuous professional development
    (CPD), 'tricks for teachers'
    forms 13
convenience sampling 47–8
critical diaries 71
critical event analysis 101–2
cultural approach 67
curriculum, information 20
curriculum development observation
    schedule 100–1

data analysis 160–73
  coding 163–6
  coherence 163
  data presentation and 143–6

atomistic approach 144
  holistic approach 144–5
evidence types 162–3
external validation 172–3
focus 163
initial research questions and 143–6
literature reviews in 164, 167, 173
methods 105–6
process 167
section in research report 178, 179
'stem and branch' 176
storage and retrieval 160–2
validity enhancement 168–73
data presentation 143–58
  and data analysis 143–6
    atomistic approach 144
    holistic approach 144–5
  initial research questions and 143–6
  qualitative data 147–8
  quantitative data 148–53
  section in research report 178, 179
  statistical test use 153–8
data recording methods 99–104
data spread 154–5
deductive method 62
degrees of freedom (df) 156
dependent variable 151
development planning 182, 183–4
diaries 85–6
  in observation 100
  pros and cons 75
dichotomous questions 90
discourse analysis 67
documents 109–23
  accessing 116–17
  assessing 115–16
  contextual 110
  definition 109–10

documents (*continued*)
  evidence analysis 122–3
  external criticism 115
  internal criticism 115
  pros and cons 75, 123
  research tool development for
      117–22
  sampling 116
  sources 109–11
  use in research 111–15
duty of care 50

educational research paradigm
    (ERP 63
emancipatory agenda 126
empiricism 62
EndNote 34
epistemology 6, 60, 62
equity 184
ethical issues 27, 50–2, 55–6, 62
  in action research 136
  guidelines 51, 52, 56
  in observation 106–7
ethnographic approaches 67
evaluation 67–8
  of lessons 112, 115
  as planning stage 184
Every Child Matters (ECM)
    agenda 21, 111
Evidence for Policy and Practice
    Information (EPPI) 33
ex post facto approach 66
executive summary 181
experimental approach 60, 66
external influences 19–21

F2F interviews 83–4
factor analysis 106

feminist research 67
filtering 167
focus, establishing 27
focus group discussion 54–5

gatekeepers 49–50
General Teaching Council for England
    (GTC) 4, 20
generalisability 168, 177
graphics, use in data presentation
    149–53
grounded theory 65–6
groups, comparing 105

'harm' 66
Harvard referencing system 179,
    180–1
Her Majesty's Inspectorate of
    Education (HMIe) 20
Higher Education Academy (HEA)
    5–6
historical approach 67
history resources example 129, 130,
    131
History Teachers Discussion Forum
    example 141–2
homework example 129, 131
host organisation, researching in 23

impact, evaluating 11–12
implementation, as planning stage 184
inclusion criteria 33
independent variable 151
indicators 18
individualised learning 10–11
inductive method 62
informed consent 56–8
'insider' research
  practitioner action research as 126
  as problematic 51

Institute for Learning and Teaching in
    Higher Education (ILTHE) 5
interaction level observation
    103, 104
internal issues 21–3
interpretive paradigm 6, 60–3
  and documents 117
inter-quartile range 155
intervention, during observation 107
interventionist approach 71
interviews
  advantages 86
  analysis 164
  case study examples 88–9
  delivery format 83–6
  pros and cons 74
  question order 176
  questionnaires vs 80
  as research tool 88–9
  schedule construction 86–8
  semi-structured 86
  structure 80–1
  structured 86
  unstructured 86–7
issues
  in educational press 18
  identifying 16–28
  internal 21–3
  national 19–21
  see also ethical issues; legal issues;
      moral issues

key informants 49, 50
key terms, finding 119
knowledge creation 136–8

Leading from the Middle (LftM) 5
learner engagement example 134

learning check 13–14
learning organisation 13
legal issues 51
lesson evaluations 112, 115
lesson plans 111–12, 113, 115
Likert scale 91
line graphs 151–3
listening skills development
    researc 63–4
literacy hour 126
literature reviews
  conceptual framework development
      using 38–40
  conducting 30–2
  conducting systematic 32–5
  in data analysis 164, 167, 173
  making more systematic 35–8
  in research report 176, 178
  search vs 30
  structure 32

maths teaching case study 120–1
mean 154
measures, relationships between 105
median 154, 155
meeting minutes 114, 115–16
mentoring
  effectiveness evaluation 26
  examples 134–5, 170–1
meta-analysis 33, 34, 106
  statistical 34
methodology, research see research
      methodology
MFL assessment example 168–70
mode 154
models of research 60–3
moral issues 51
MsAccess 34

MsPowerpoint presentations case
    stud 121–2
MsWord 119
multi-disciplinary research 137
multiple-choice questions 90–1

narrative approach 70
narrative empirical synthesis 34
narrative flow 176
National College for School
    Leadership (NCSL) 4, 20, 21
National Curriculum levels, as
    standards 185
national issues 19–21
National Professional Qualification for
    Headship (NPQH) 4
naturalistic approach 60
non-probability sampling 47–8
note-taking 84
NQT induction example 165–6
NUD*IST 34, 162
null hypotheses 155
N-Vivo 34, 162

observation 95–108
  data analysis methods 105–6
  data recording methods
      99–104
  ethical issues 106–7
  flexibility 96
  highly structured 98
  intervention during 107
  as 'natural' research tool 96
  pros and cons 73, 97
  semi-structured 98
  systematic approach 102–3
  types and forms 97–9
  unstructured 98

Ofsted 11, 100
  resources 20
online interviews 85
online questionnaires 83
ontology 60, 61
open-ended questions 90, 93
open minds 25–6
outliers 154
ownership 52–3, 127, 184, 187

paradigms 6, 60
participant
  complete 98, 99
  marginal 98–9
  as observer 98
  observer-as- 99
participant information sheets 56–7
participatory action research
      (PAR 128
peer validation 173
performance targets 184–5, 186
personal development plans (PDP) 11
personal professional development,
      strength 10
PGCE 4
PGDE 4
phenomenological approach 6–7
pie charts 149–50
plan-teach-assess/evaluate-plan cycl 66
planning cycle 184
policy documents 112
populations
  comparing data from different 155–8
  definition 46
positionality 22, 26, 61
positivist paradigm 6, 25, 60–3
  and documents 117

post compulsory education (PCE)
    sector 5
postgraduate certificate of education
    (PGCE) 4
postgraduate profession, move
    toward 4–6
postgraduate professional development
    (PPD) 4
practitioners, researchers vs 59
prediction 106
probability sampling 46–7
process targets 186
professional graduate diploma in
    education (PGDE) 4
pros and cons, working from 72–6
protocol, review 33
pupil behaviour example 134
purposive sampling 47

qualified teacher status (QTS) 4
qualitative data 146–7, 162
    presentation 147–8
qualitative methodology 63, 106
quantitative data 146–7, 162
    presentation 148–53
quantitative methodology 63, 106
questionnaires
    constructing 89–93
    delivery format 81–3
    interviews vs 80
    pros and cons 74
    as research tool 93–4
    structure 80–1
questions
    asking 24–5
    deconstructing 68–72
    generic 69–72
    types 89–93
quota sampling 47

random sampling 47
range 154
    inter-quartile 155
rank order 90, 91–2
rating scales 90, 91
ratio data 90, 93
rationale 61
reality check 27–8
reconnaissance 130, 132, 133
recording units 117
reference management software 34
Reference Manager 34
referencing 179, 180–1
reflective practice 6–7, 58, 125–6
    action research and 125–6
    as four-stage model 7
regression analysis 106
reliability 168
reports, research see research reports
research
    purpose of 17–18, 175
        clarifying 27–8
research activity, level of engagement
        with 14
research approaches 64–8
research design 16
research informed practice 6–7
research location
    host organisation 23
    own organisation 23
research methodology 73–6
    qualitative 63, 106
    quantitative 63, 106
    section in research report 177, 178
    selection vs de-selection 76–7
research models 60–3
research processes, teaching processes
        vs 8–10

research reports
   conclusion section 178, 179, 181
   referencing 179, 180–1
   structure 175–9
   to non-specialist audiences 179, 181–2
research terminology 65
research tools 77
   and data storage and retrieval 162
   for documents 117–22
   in observation 99–104
researchers, practitioners vs 59
responsive evaluation 68
risk assessment 62

sampling 46–8
   of documentation 116
scatter graphs 151, 152
scholarly skills 179
school improvement model 184, 185–6
school improvement plans (SIPs) 11
school performance targets 184–5, 186
science subject leader case studies 114, 118–19
scientific paradigm *see* positivist paradigm
search
   exhaustive 33
   review vs 30
self-evaluation forms (SEFs) 11
self-validation 173
settings, gathering data on 97–8
significance levels 155
SMART targets 186
snowball sampling 47
social constructivism 9, 136

socialisation level observation 103, 104
source identification 148
speaking skills development research 63–4
Spearman's rank 91, 157–8
sports college case study 113–14
spreadsheets 148
standard deviation 154
starting points 25
statistical significance 155
statistical tests 153–8
strategy 182–3
   definition 182
   translation into action 183
stratified sampling 47
subjectivity 62, 168
surveys 67, 79–80
   case studies and 78, 80
   question order 176
SWOT analysis 82
syntheses 34–5
   conceptual 34–5
   narrative empirical 34
systematic reviews
   characteristics 33–4
   conducting 32–5
   document 37, 38
   toolkit 35, 36
systems analysis 67–8

tables, use in data presentation 148–9
targets
   process 186
   school performance 184–5, 186
   SMART 186
Teacher Learning Academy (TLA) 4
Teachernet 19

teaching
  action research and 135–6
  as evidence-based profession 187
  move toward postgraduate profession
      4–6
teaching assistants (TAs)
  development example 171–2
  in target setting 184
teaching processes, research processes
      vs 8–10
telephone interviews 84–5
television programmes, as
      documentation source 111
tests, pros and cons 76
textual analysis 122
time off-task observation 103, 104
tracking, dynamic 11–12
Training and Development Agency for
      schools (TDA) 4, 20
transferability 168

triangulation 167, 170–2
trustworthiness 168

up-liner validation 173

validity 168
  enhancing 168–73
  external validation 172–3
  internal 168
video conferencing 84
video recording 84
  of class 113
virtual learning environments 83
vision 184
voluntary participation 56
volunteer sampling 47–8

web logs 86
withdrawal, right to 56
workforce remodelling 184